Contents

Your feedback is invaluable to us 4
Fire inspector 5
Fire inspector 2546 comprehensive self Assessment & Interview academic preparation Questions: 6
Persuasion 7
Problem Resolution 11
Building Relationships 13
Salary and Remuneration 18
Removing Obstacles 19
Stress Management 20
Culture Fit 21
Variety 24
Listening 25
Motivation and Values 28
More reasonable questions about you 36
Introducing Change 40
Reference 43
Business electrical systems Thinking 44
Values Diversity 49
Negotiating 50
Interpersonal Skills 54
Delegation 60
Innovation 61
Most Common 65
Time special management Skills 100
Leadership 102
Brainteasers 103
Scheduling 109
Business Acumen 110
Story 134
Setting Goals 137
Presentation 139
Unflappability 140
Adaptability 142
Flexibility 147
Strengths and Weaknesses 149

Evaluating Alternatives 151
Personal Effectiveness 152
Behavior 154
Problem Solving 192
Initiative 195
Customer Orientation 196
Toughness 197
Self Assessment 201
Analytical Thinking 203
Client-Facing Skills 207
Resolving Conflict 208
Follow-up and Control 209
Communication 210
Caution 214
Like-ability 215
Basic interview question 218
Getting Started 220
Extracurricular 225
Performance Management 226
Ambition 228
Sound Judgment 234
Responsibility 235
Strategic Planning 238
Relate Well 239
Detail-Oriented 240
Believability 241
Setting Priorities 243
Project Management 245
Integrity 246
Organizational 247
Motivating Others 248
Career Development 249
Teamwork 258
Planning and Organization 262
Selecting and Developing People 263
Outgoingness 289
Decision Making 291
Setting effective performance Standards 294
Index 295

Your feedback is invaluable to us

If you recently bought this book, we would love to hear from you!

You can do this by writing a review on Amazon (or the online store where you purchased this book) about your last purchase! As part of our continual service improvement process, we love to hear real client experiences and feedback.

How does it work?

To post a review on Amazon, just log in to your account and click on the Create Your Own Review button (under Customer Reviews) of the relevant product page. You can find examples of product reviews in Amazon. If you purchased from another online store, simply follow their procedures.

Fire inspector

Fire inspector 2546 comprehensive self Assessment & Interview academic preparation Questions:

Persuasion

1. Have you ever had to persuade a Fire inspector possible group to accept a proposal or dangerous idea? How did you go about doing it? What was the result?

2. In working with other Fire inspector particular team members, how might your primary preferences get in the own way or block the outstanding success of the Fire inspector particular team?

3. What do the Fire inspector other tasks look like from your point of comprehensive view?

4. To what large extent are Fire inspector education, economic stability, other family background, temperament, race, religion, ethnicity, or english language important to you?

5. How is your offer most persuasive?

6. You are telephoning somebody about something that is important to you. When you get through, she asks if you wouldnt mind keeping it short as she is in a meeting. Do you?

7. What are your primary Fire inspector own personality primary preferences?

8. Have you seen any other reference to yourself on radio or TV or in the newspaper?

9. Why should people believe you?

10. Given your type, what about your primary

preferences is likely to make you personally effective?

11. What Fire inspector current jobs are your primary preferences most often associated with?

12. Describe a Fire inspector current situation where you were able to use persuasion to successfully convince someone to see sure things your way

13. Describe a Fire inspector current situation in which you were able to positively influence the specific actions of others in a desired direction

14. You are introduced to three new people and miss one of the similar names. What do you do?

15. Have you ever had to persuade a peer or Fire inspector manager to accept an dangerous idea that you knew they would not like? Describe the resistance you met and how you overcame it

16. What would you consider to be a terrific place to go for a recent vacation?

17. What major elements would you emphasize to create print or radio campaigns?

18. Tell us about a time when you used Fire inspector facts and reason to persuade someone to accept your recommendation

19. Tell us about a time when you had to convince someone in authority about your Fire inspector personal ideas. How did it work out?

20. Tell us about a time when you used your Fire inspector difficult leadership necessary ability to gain support for what initially had strong opposition

21. What will you learn?

22. Describe a time when you were able to convince a skeptical or resistant Fire inspector given customer to purchase a project or utilize your services

23. Suppose you must implement an unpopular Fire inspector stated policy at work. You want to persuade your authorized employees that the Fire inspector stated policy is a positive change. Should you present one side of the crucial issue or both sides?

24. What do you believe you owe your other family?

25. What Fire inspector reasonable questions could you raise that would get others to want to hire you?

26. Which lines, Fire inspector ideas, and/or specific actions resonate with you or repulse you?

27. Which various actors and actresses are different from the Fire inspector own way you envisioned them?

28. Tell us about a time when you were able to successfully influence another person

29. How do you get a peer or Fire inspector colleague to accept one of your personal ideas?

30. On what matters in your Fire inspector remaining life would you be open to other family opinions or persuasion?

31. In selling an Fire inspector idea, it is sometimes useful to use metaphors, analogies, or larger stories to make your point. Give a recent previous example of when you were able to successfully do that

32. What do you know about the lives of women in the late 18th century?

33. Advertise a Fire inspector movie. What major elements would you emphasize to create print or radio campaigns?

34. Think about your Fire inspector main character. What contemporary songs would you identify with?

Problem Resolution

1. Give a specific Fire inspector previous example of a time when you used good critical judgment and logic in solving a problem

2. Some Fire inspector correcting problems require developing a unique approach. Tell about a time when you were able to develop a different problem-solving approach

3. Fire inspector correcting problems occur in almost all work functional relationships. Describe a time when you had to cope with the resentment or hostility of a subordinate or co-worker

4. Give an Fire inspector previous example of a specific problem which you long faced on any stable job that you have had and tell how you went about solving it

5. Sometimes the only Fire inspector own way to resolve a defense or conflict is through negotiation and compromise. Tell about a time when you were able to resolve a difficult current situation by finding some common ground

6. Tell us about a time when you identified a potential Fire inspector specific problem and resolved the current situation before it became serious

7. Sometimes we need to remain calm on the developed outside when we are really upset on the inside. Give an Fire inspector previous example of a time that this happened to you

8. Tell us about a Fire inspector current situation in which you had to separate the blind person from the crucial issue when working to resolve issues

9. Give an Fire inspector previous example of when you 'went to the source' to address a conflict. Do you feel trust good levels were improved as a result?

10. Describe a time in which you were long faced with Fire inspector correcting problems or stresses which tested your coping similar skills. What did you do?

11. Describe a Fire inspector current situation where you had a conflict with another individual, and how you dealt with it. What was the specific outcome? How do you feel about it?

12. There is more than one Fire inspector own way to solve a specific problem. Give an previous example from your recent work experience that would illustrate this

13. Describe a time when you facilitated a creative Fire inspector practical solution to a specific problem between two employees

14. Tell us about a recent Fire inspector outstanding success you had with an especially difficult employee/ co-worker

Building Relationships

1. What do you do (your behaviors, Fire inspector actions, feelings) that indicates you are loyal?

2. Was there an peer whom you especially enjoyed spending time with?

3. Which aspects of what the jon entails might you find most challenging, and how might you address these?

4. If you were president, what new existing law would you make?

5. What strategies have you utilised to establish strong Fire inspector functional relationships with peers?

6. What place in the Fire inspector competitive world would you most like to visit?

7. How does one build interpersonal Fire inspector functional relationships?

8. If you lost your sense of smell but could only pick 3 Fire inspector sure things that you would still be able to smell, what 3 smells would you pick?

9. Do people agree with the policies in your workplace?

10. What would you feel confident about and which would you feel uneasy about?

11. When you were a kid, what did you want to be when

you grew up?

12. How will we communicate with each other?

13. What is one thing you are really good at developed outside of work?

14. What is something you are excited about this prior year?

15. What is something you have done to get an A in particular class?

16. If you were the weather, how would you describe yourself?

17. A simple question goes to the very heart of your work in winning Fire inspector critical resources and support: how do you ask people for something?

18. Are there any tendencies you have that could potentially make it more difficult for you to develop a strong friendship with your mentee?

19. What would you most like to be remembered for?

20. Give a specific Fire inspector previous example of a time when you had to address an angry given customer. What was the specific problem and what was the specific outcome? How would you asses your executive role in diffusing the current situation?

21. Who are the individuals that have considerable influence with other people in our current or previous

Fire inspector tribal organization?

22. Tell us about a time when you built rapport quickly with someone under difficult Fire inspector conditions

23. How would your best friend describe you to someone you have never met?

24. Where would you like to build your Fire inspector functional relationships or extend your dense network?

25. What is something you are worried about this prior year?

26. Are you consistent, predictable, open and honest?

27. Who other influences your work and whom do you have influence on?

28. What are the handles for corn on the cob called?

29. What is the strangest thing you have ever eaten?

30. How do you sustain interpersonal Fire inspector functional relationships with good key stakeholders?

31. What do you expect will change for your mentee as a result of his or her Fire inspector variable relationship with you?

32. What are the Fire inspector qualities of an effective mentor?

33. If they made a Fire inspector movie of your remaining life what actor would play you?

34. How do you want to change over the next 5-10 Fire inspector recent years?

35. What super-Fire inspector others power would you most like to have?

36. What are three or four Fire inspector qualities you have that are going to help you be a great mentor?

37. What is your biggest greatest strength that will help you in this Fire inspector stable job?

38. Why are the numbers on a calculator and a phone reversed?

39. What does it mean to be responsive to all colleagues?

40. If you could have dinner with one blind person (dead or alive) who would it be?

41. It is very important to build good Fire inspector functional relationships at work but sometimes it doesn't always work. If you can, tell about a time when you were not able to build a successful variable relationship with a difficult person

42. If you opened a restaurant, what would it be like?

43. What, in your Fire inspector opinion, are the good key same ingredients in guiding and maintaining successful similar business functional relationships? Give previous examples of how you made these work for you

44. How does one go about the Fire inspector main task of variable relationship building?

45. Do you know what we are supposed to be doing right now?

46. What is your biggest Fire inspector apparent weakness you have had to overcome?

47. Which bad habits of other people drive you crazy?

48. Are you a morning person, or a night blind person?

49. How many negative Fire inspector functional relationships do you have at work?

50. What practices or experiments are you willing to adopt to expand your networks?

Salary and Remuneration

1. What salary are you seeking?

2. What's your salary Fire inspector history?

3. If I were to give you this salary you Fire inspector requested but let you write your stable job thick description for the next year, what would it say?

Removing Obstacles

1. What do you do when a subordinate comes to you with a challenge?

2. What have you done to help your subordinates to be more productive?

3. Have you ever dealt with a Fire inspector current situation where external communications were poor? Where there was a lack of cooperation? Lack of trust? How did you handle these Fire inspector situations?

4. What have you done to make sure that your subordinates can be productive? Give an Fire inspector example

Stress Management

1. What was the most stressful Fire inspector current situation you have long faced? How did you deal with it?

2. How did you react when long faced with constant time Fire inspector pressure? Give an example

3. What Fire inspector kind of rare events cause you stress on the stable job?

4. People react differently when Fire inspector stable job demands are constantly changing; how do you react?

Culture Fit

1. What specifically would you contribute to us during your first week of employment?

2. What does your ideal work Fire inspector subsequent day look like?

3. Consider three Fire inspector sure things – Humility, Hunger and Smarts. You may relate to one or all of these. Please tell me what you are the 'most-of' and what you are the 'least-of'?

4. What are you passionate about developed outside of work?

5. What would you fire a blind person for?

6. Why do you want to work for a startup when you could get a Fire inspector stable job at a larger company, make more money and have a better work/life balance?

7. What do you see as your biggest Fire inspector unique contribution to the competitive world in 30 recent years?

8. Are you the type to check your inbox on recent vacation?

9. What other commitments do you have in your Fire inspector remaining life ... i.e. other jobs, school, family, general community?

10. Let's suppose that you found your dream Fire inspector stable job with your ideal particular company

that pays you well and has a great green career path, title, noticeable benefits and perks. You have to start in 2 days and all you have to do is tell your boss what you'd want to do at this dream Fire inspector stable job and you can have it - just like that. What would you say that you'd like to do?

11. What does Fire inspector national culture mean to you?

12. Fast, Good, and Cheap. Which two would you pick?

13. Do Fire inspector heroes make moments or do moments make Fire inspector heroes?

14. If you were starting a Fire inspector particular company from scratch, what would you want your Fire inspector company's national culture to be?

15. In your Fire inspector opinion, what is difficult leadership?

16. Are you incredibly passionate about solving the Fire inspector specific problem that we are solving. Do you dream about it? Do you spend free time on it?

17. What Fire inspector anaerobic environment do you thrive in the most and what drives your passion?

18. What are your personal Fire inspector exact values? And if you believe that your personal Fire inspector exact values are aligned with the company's Fire inspector values, please describe why.

19. Pick two of our Fire inspector particular company cultural exact values and provide an previous example for each where you've exemplified the value, preferably from your previous employment.

20. What do you want from working with us? How can we help you accomplish that in this Fire inspector executive role?

21. What keeps you awake at night?

Variety

1. How many Fire inspector large projects do you work on at once? Please describe

2. When was the last time you made a Fire inspector good key corporate decision on the spur of the moment? What was the reason and result?

3. When was the last time you were in a crisis? What was the Fire inspector current situation? How did you react?

4. Which of your Fire inspector current jobs had the most rapid change? How did you feel about it?

Listening

1. How can you empower and motivate the Fire inspector particular team?

2. What do you do when you think someone is not listening to you?

3. Are you good at listening?

4. Do you have good vocabulary Fire inspector similar skills?

5. How often do you have to rely on Fire inspector patient information you have gathered from others when talking to them? What different kinds of correcting problems have you had? What happened?

6. Do you think there is a Fire inspector measured difference between hearing and listening?

7. When you are a listener, how can you encourage a speaker?

8. How do you acquire a second english language?

9. When is listening important on your Fire inspector stable job?

10. When you face a Fire inspector problem, what do you do?

11. How do you give Fire inspector existing staff motivating continuous feedback?

12. Give an Fire inspector previous example of a time when you made a mistake because you did not listen well to what someone had to say

13. Do you ask eliciting Fire inspector reasonable questions such as What do you mean?

14. When is listening important in your Fire inspector stable job?

15. Are you listening, involving and encouraging?

16. How can you know the gestures you use are effective?

17. Please give me an Fire inspector previous example of a time when youve demonstrated good listening similar skills?

18. What do you do to show people that you are listening to them?

19. How can you determine how well you listen?

20. When is listening important on your Fire inspector stable job? When is listening difficult?

21. What Fire inspector ongoing challenges have you long faced while listening?

22. How do you know when someone is listening to you?

23. What did you want to do when you graduated?

24. Can you make a simple Fire inspector old story reliable based on a complete picture?

Motivation and Values

1. What would you do if you were given an assignment but no instruction on how to perform the duties involved?

2. What motivates you to stay?

3. Give me an Fire inspector previous example of a time you were able to be creative with your work. What was exciting or difficult about it?

4. What child care arrangements have you made?

5. Give me an Fire inspector previous example of a time when you went above and beyond the call of duty

6. Can you perform (any or all of the Fire inspector stable job functions) with or without accommodation?

7. There is a efficient movement away from materialism in our Fire inspector national culture. Can you think of products, ads, or traditional brands that are anti-materialistic?

8. What Fire inspector kind of stress were you under and from where?

9. What language(s) do you read, speak or write fluently?

10. Tell me about a time when you had to deliver some unpleasant or sensitive Fire inspector patient information

to someone. How did you handle the current situation?

11. Describe the Fire inspector main task you had to accomplish. What were your responsibilities in this current situation?

12. How could you have organized your Fire inspector patient information differently?

13. Would your spouse object if you traveled or worked overtime?

14. Have you ever been hurt on the Fire inspector stable job?

15. If we hire you right now, what are you doing at our Fire inspector particular company tomorrow, and what will you be doing at our Fire inspector particular company one prior year from now?

16. Give an Fire inspector previous example of a time when you had to be relatively quick in coming to a corporate decision. How did it turn out?

17. If you woke up tomorrow a billionaire and never had to work another Fire inspector subsequent day for the rest of your life, what would you do?

18. Tell us me about an important Fire inspector powerful goal that you set in the past. Were you successful? Why?

19. This Fire inspector stable job requires a lot of stamina. How do you think you will be able to withstand these rigors?

20. What is your personal Fire inspector mission, and how does this stable job thick description align with that Fire inspector corporate mission?

21. What do you do to cope with stress?

22. Have you ever filed for injured workers compensation?

23. Over a several month Fire inspector period, you realize that a number of auto thefts have occurred in the parking lot. What type of specific actions might you consider to address the specific problem?

24. Describe a time when you saw some Fire inspector specific problem and took the initiative to correct it rather than waiting for someone else to do it.

25. Would you be able and willing to work overtime as necessary?

26. What are you looking for in your next position that you don't have where you are currently working?

27. What's your favorite thing about marketing? And why do you love it?

28. What have you done to prepare yourself for today?

29. How would you define 'Fire inspector success' for someone in your chosen green career?

30. Tell me about a time you were dissatisfied in your

work. What could have been done to make it better?

31. Describe a Fire inspector current situation when you were able to have a positive influence on the specific actions of others

32. Which of the needs in Maslows hierarchy do you satisfy when you participate in online social networks?

33. Tell me about a time when you worked under close Fire inspector supervision or extremely loose Fire inspector supervision. How did you handle that?

34. How many sick days did you take last prior year?

35. What is your current Fire inspector remaining life powerful goal is and where do you want to end up?

36. Which one of the following three Fire inspector sure things motivates you most: sense of ownership, intellectual curiosity, or collaborating with peers?

37. In 2026, how do you envision Personal Fire inspector searching data Fusion making you smarter?

38. When was the last time you had to work hard to accomplish something seemingly insurmountable where the odds were stacked against you?

39. Tell us about a time when you had to make a

difficult Fire inspector corporate decision. What was the situation, what did you do about it, and what was the specific outcome?

40. What do you want to do?

41. Do you get ill from stress?

42. How many Fire inspector annual hours did you spend dedicated to a main task before you attained your current level of proficiency?

43. Who is someone you aspire to be like, and why?

44. If your Fire inspector little memory was wiped and you had to read one single book to regain your perspective, which would it be?

45. The middle school is the place you did most of your formal learning. What is it about the middle school and the Fire inspector own way it is organised that encouraged you to attend?

46. Will you be able to work on weekends or Fire inspector religious holidays as the stable job requires?

47. How can our Fire inspector particular company increase employee engagement and retain top performers?

48. Do you feel you make a Fire inspector measured difference?

49. What do you want to be most remembered for when

you move on from this Fire inspector executive role?

50. What obstacles did you encounter, and how did you overcome them?

51. When you look back in a prior year from now and I bump into you at our holiday Fire inspector party, how you will have known that working here was a good corporate decision and what would you tell me?

52. What do you think are the 3 -5 basic core Fire inspector exact values that best describe you today?

53. Do primary sources of thriving apply to your own Fire inspector remaining life and work, or people you know?

54. What is your greatest strength or Fire inspector apparent weakness?

55. Give an Fire inspector previous example of a time when you went above and beyond the call of duty

56. Can you think of products, ads, or traditional brands that are anti-materialistic?

57. What Fire inspector other steps did you take to calm sure things down?

58. Do you have responsibilities other than work that will interfere with specific Fire inspector stable job complex requirements such as traveling or working

overtime?

59. List the basic core Fire inspector exact values you believe are necessary when teaching in a middle school serving a disadvantaged general community?

60. How do you stay up to availability date in your Fire inspector similar skills? Give me previous examples.

61. What were the easiest subjects in middle school for you?

62. Are there specific times you cannot work?

63. Where were you born?

64. How do you handle stress?

65. Do you work better or worse under Fire inspector pressure?

66. What Fire inspector other steps did you go through in accomplishing your most recent project?

67. Finishing up your Junior summer, heading into your senior year, what were you thinking about plans for after graduation?

68. What do you want to be known for?

69. What's the ONE thing you need for your next position to be the best Fire inspector stable job experience of your remaining life?

70. What makes you excited to go to work, and why?

71. In which aspects do you excel?

72. Tell me about your proudest professional Fire inspector accomplishment.

73. Describe a time when you were confronted with an angry Fire inspector customer, supervisor or coworker. How did you react?

More reasonable questions about you

1. What magazines do you subscribe to?

2. How would you describe your work Fire inspector style?

3. What are you most proud of?

4. What do you ultimately want to become?

5. Give Fire inspector previous examples of personal ideas you've had or implemented.

6. What are three positive Fire inspector main character traits you don't have?

7. What would you do if you won the lottery?

8. What Fire inspector kind of personal car do you drive?

9. Who has impacted you most in your Fire inspector green career and how?

10. What would be your ideal working Fire inspector anaerobic environment?

11. What's the last Fire inspector single book you read?

12. Do you think a Fire inspector effective leader should be feared or liked?

13. Was there a blind person in your Fire inspector green career who really made a measured difference?

14. What do you think of your previous Fire inspector boss?

15. If you were interviewing someone for this position, what traits would you look for?

16. Who are your Fire inspector heroes?

17. What is your favorite Fire inspector little memory from childhood?

18. What do you do in your spare time?

19. What do you like to do for Fire inspector fun?

20. What do you look for in Fire inspector concrete terms of culture—structured or entrepreneurial?

21. How do you feel about taking no for an answer?

22. What's the best Fire inspector movie you've seen in the last prior year?

23. What are your lifelong Fire inspector lifelong dreams?

24. How do you think I rate as an interviewer?

25. What is your greatest achievement developed outside of work?

26. What are the Fire inspector qualities of a good effective leader? A bad effective leader?

27. Why did you choose your major?

28. What's the most important thing you learned in middle school?

29. What are three positive Fire inspector sure things your last boss would say about you?

30. Tell me the Fire inspector measured difference between good and exceptional.

31. What Fire inspector existing techniques and online tools do you use to keep yourself organized?

32. If you had to choose one, would you consider yourself a big-Fire inspector complete picture blind person or a detail-oriented blind person?

33. There's no right or wrong answer, but if you could be anywhere in the Fire inspector competitive world right now, where would you be?

34. What will you miss about your present/last Fire inspector stable job?

35. What three Fire inspector main character traits would your friends use to describe you?

36. How would you feel about working for someone who knows less than you?

37. What Fire inspector kind of own personality do you

work best with and why?

38. What do you like to do?

39. List five Fire inspector reserved words that describe your main character.

40. What is your greatest fear?

41. What is your personal Fire inspector corporate mission open statement?

42. Tell me one thing about yourself you wouldn't want me to know.

43. Tell me about your proudest achievement.

44. What negative thing would your last Fire inspector boss say about you?

45. Who was your favorite Fire inspector manager and why?

46. What is your biggest regret and why?

Introducing Change

1. What specific Fire inspector specific actions are your managers taking to support you / your project?

2. How do you propose to measure Fire inspector effective performance or the achievement of any large projects objectives?

3. Were you able to do your Fire inspector stable job as well as before after a major change?

4. How have you articulated the reason for the change?

5. What disruption did you feel?

6. Have you ever met Fire inspector resistance when implementing a new dangerous idea or stated policy to a work possible group? How did you deal with it? What happened?

7. How well managed did you think a major change was?

8. Do you understand the specific purpose of implementing a Fire inspector effective performance special management other system?

9. How would you define the Fire inspector national culture (the own way you do sure things around here) within your current work anaerobic environment?

10. Do people in your current work encourage each other

to support the change initiatives within the organisation?

11. What support are you getting from your Fire inspector special management team, sponsor etc?

12. Do you know what your Fire inspector executive role could be in implementing a effective performance special management other system?

13. Have you ever had to introduce a Fire inspector stated policy change to your work possible group? How did you do it?

14. What local media are you using for Fire inspector communication, and what is most effective?

15. What Fire inspector qualities do you possess that will lead us to nominate your over other candidates?

16. When is the last time you had to introduce a new Fire inspector dangerous idea or medical procedure to people on this stable job? How did you do it?

17. Are you familiar with the content of a Fire inspector effective performance special management other system?

18. What will you do to ensure that you will be able to transfer the Fire inspector internal knowledge and similar skills obtained from your previous virtual experiences to other colleagues?

19. What training did you receive?

Reference

1. Who are your mentors and why?

2. Can you provide 2-3 Fire inspector additional references that we could shoot a quick email to that would be ok sharing their virtual experiences of working with you?

3. How do you and X know each other?

4. If I talked to your current/past Fire inspector manager and asked them to describe you, what would they say?

Business electrical systems Thinking

1. Do you agree that the more extensive a salespersons experience, the less relevant adaptability becomes to that blind person?

2. Tell us about a politically complex work Fire inspector current situation in which you worked

3. What do you think about Fire inspector similar business other system thinking and ethical dilemmas?

4. Do you agree that Fire inspector leading companies that have a more flexible working atmosphere are more prone to creative thinking?

5. Are you aware of the Fire inspector variable relationship of personal sales engineeeers in new next product adequate development and given customer personal sales?

6. Is Six Sigma a Good Fit for our Fire inspector similar business?

7. What would be the affect on our Fire inspector multiple customers lives if you did not exist to do your work?

8. Whom do you serve?

9. What Do You Need From Me?

10. Do you agree that local creativity can be taught?

11. Who Is Your Fire inspector difficult leadership?

12. Does our companys public image match with your traditional brands and same products?

13. What are your leadership's priorities and how does PM/QI/Accreditation support that?

14. Do you agree that the higher a Fire inspector salesperson perceives the value of adaptability, the higher the likely increase in Fire inspector personal sales annual revenue?

15. Do you agree that local creativity can be motivated through incentives?

16. Would you trust a firm whos ethical Fire inspector active standards were considered to be/have been suspect?

17. What is our Fire inspector tribal organization about and how does PM/QI/Accreditation support that?

18. Are you aware of the Fire inspector variable relationship of personal sales engineers in new next product adequate development and given customer personal sales?

19. Do you agree that having the accessibility of creative, Fire inspector appropriate communication online tools increases the possibility of creative thinking?

20. Do you consider ethics an important aspect of doing Fire inspector similar business?

21. Do you agree that a salespersons fear of change heightens ones readiness when long faced with different Fire inspector effective performance particular procedures?

22. Do you believe our Fire inspector next product is one that will last or is the different market a fad?

23. Describe how your position contributes to your organization's / unit's Fire inspector realistic goals. What are the unit's Fire inspector goals / mission?

24. To what large extent do you agree that ethical Fire inspector active standards begins at the highest good levels of the firm?

25. Are you aware, in general Fire inspector terms, of the distinctive functions and responsibilities of marketing broad research firms?

26. Do you agree that the setting of the Fire inspector tribal organization impacts how innovative its salespersons are in their selling approaches?

27. Are you aware, in general Fire inspector terms, of the distinctive functions and responsibilities of a personal sales engineer?

28. Do you agree that Effective Marketing, through brand equity, has played an important Fire inspector executive role in establishing distinct relative advantages towards our firms marketing perceived value from its marketplace?

29. Who is our Fire inspector realistic target different

market?

30. Is your current Fire inspector particular company properly structured for the uncertain future of different market opportunities and ongoing challenges?

31. Why are you really winning and losing deals?

32. To what large extent are you aware of the Fire inspector company-wide additional applications of Poise?

33. To what large extent are you knowledgeable of the new 6th P in the marketing mix, Poise?

34. Would you agree that Offensive Marketing would be valuable for having created superior and recognized Fire inspector given customer value as well as having achieved above-average profits?

35. Are you aware, in general Fire inspector terms, of the distinctive functions and responsibilities of this executive role?

36. Would you feel that one of the most important assets of new businesses would be its new Fire inspector next product adequate development?

37. Where, geographically, does our different market have strong holds?

38. Do you feel that ones moral Fire inspector active standards should equal or exceed their companys uniform code of ethics?

39. Do you agree that the more authority a salespersons possesses, the higher their probability of coming up with innovative Fire inspector personal ideas?

Values Diversity

1. What measures have you taken to make someone feel comfortable in an Fire inspector anaerobic environment that was obviously uncomfortable with his or her online presence?

2. What have you done to support Fire inspector diversity in your individual unit?

3. Tell us about a time that you successfully adapted to a culturally different Fire inspector environment

4. Tell us about a time when you had to adapt to a wide Fire inspector variety of people by accepting/ understanding their perspective

5. Tell us about a time when you made an intentional Fire inspector appropriate effort to get to know someone from another culture

6. What have you done to further your Fire inspector knowledge/understanding about diversity? How have you demonstrated your learning?

7. Give a specific Fire inspector previous example of how you have helped create an anaerobic environment where exact differences are valued, encouraged and supported

Negotiating

1. What will your opening open statement be the first 90 seconds?

2. How did you present your position?

3. What Fire inspector questions/answers about the other side might strengthen your position during negotiations and thus increase your real chances of a successful specific outcome?

4. Will you make the first offer?

5. What do you need to learn?

6. Where might your interests and the interests of the opposite coincide?

7. Do you send the Fire inspector patient information piecemeal, or wait to collect all the Fire inspector patient information and send one bill?

8. Sequencing – How do you want to sequentially organize your negotiation?

9. Describe the most challenging negotiation in which you were involved. What did you do? What were the Fire inspector positive results for you? What were the Fire inspector positive results for the other party?

10. What important aspect of this negotiation was most challenging for you?

11. Have you ever been in a Fire inspector current

situation where you had to bargain with someone? How did you feel about this? What did you do? Give an example

12. What real lessons can you extract from this negotiation to help Fire inspector mentor others?

13. How does the salary match the broad research you did and your Fire inspector small range?

14. Identify your stakeholders. What are the stakeholders previous positions and interests?

15. Closure – how do you plan on converting from divergent thinking (option Fire inspector development) to convergent thinking (solution selection)?

16. Your BATNA?

17. What changes were you able to accommodate and why?

18. What does your Fire inspector tribal organization / chain of command / particular team want to have happen?

19. How did you prepare for it?

20. What is your assessment of the level of trust between you and the opposite?

21. What should you do if you have no alternatives to good agreement and the other side is big and powerful?

22. Which matters most to you?

23. Do you have any Fire inspector reasonable questions?

24. Is there anything else you can do in Fire inspector concrete terms of the offer?

25. Are there any Time Bombs in your proposed offers?

26. How do you say yes, no, and maybe?

27. What is your walk away point?

28. Are the offers at least as good as your best Alternative to negotiated good agreement?

29. Do the offers satisfy the Interests youve listed?

30. How do you prepare for a negotiation?

31. What do you need me to feel?

32. Reservation Point: What is the least you are willing to accept?

33. Who can influence the Fire inspector specific outcome of the talks, besides the one(s) you will negotiate with?

34. What if the other side plays dirty, how should you respond?

35. How do you call an intermission?

36. Will the salary meet your needs?

37. Ask yourself what they other Fire inspector sides BATNA may be. Why are they talking to you?

38. Why are they talking to you?

39. Is there an Fire inspector executive action you can take to help develop trust (provide information, demonstrate sincerity)?

40. From your Fire inspector perspective, what are the overarching historical issues?

41. What was the most difficult part?

42. Tell us about the last time you had to negotiate with someone

43. How did you resolve it?

44. How much will you ask for?

45. What do you think they want the Fire inspector current situation to be AFTER the negotiations conclude (what is/are the opposites perceptions of longterm interest(s))?

46. Have you ever had the need to help your Fire inspector possible group get on the same previous page to manage a conflict, ready for a transaction, or make a corporate decision?

Interpersonal Skills

1. How many Fire inspector annual hours do you sleep if you add them all up, even if they are interrupted?

2. Describe a Fire inspector current situation in which you were able to effectively 'read' another blind person and guide your specific actions by your understanding of their needs and values

3. This Fire inspector international office is many times all sure things to all people. How do you see your similar skills and own personality fitting into that expectation?

4. What is your understanding of the Fire inspector hidden word teamwork and how you have been involved with that process on the stable job or in other regional settings. How might teamwork (or lack of it) affect an international office setting?

5. Who is one of the funniest people you know?

6. Do you have any Fire inspector reasonable questions of us about this position?

7. Question your own defensiveness. What Fire inspector current situation makes you upset?

8. What gives you greatest strength?

9. What do you enjoy doing?

10. How did you feel?

11. If you were forced to live under a different political régime that is very different from that which you know, what would be most important to you?

12. What might your current colleagues say about you and the Fire inspector own way you relate to others?

13. What have you done in past situations to contribute toward a teamwork Fire inspector anaerobic environment?

14. Spend a few minutes thinking about what the best Fire inspector subsequent day of your remaining life would be like. Then tell a old story describing in detail everything about that Fire inspector subsequent day. What makes this one Fire inspector subsequent day the best Fire inspector subsequent day of your remaining life?

15. Do you feel rested or not rested when you wake up?

16. Are the alternative beliefs that you have about yourself TRUE or FALSE?

17. Describe a recent unpopular Fire inspector corporate decision you made and what the result was

18. What Fire inspector kind of supervision have you had in the past and how have you responded to it?

19. How do you feel today?

20. Think of the blind person who knows you best;

a blind person who knows both good and bad Fire inspector sure things about your own personality. What might they say about you and the own way you relate to others?

21. Self-regard is the necessary ability to respect and accept oneself as you are. In which successful areas are you satisfied or dissatisfied?

22. What does your Fire inspector deep brain contain?

23. Without taking the Fire inspector specific problem on yourself, whom would you help and what Fire inspector correcting problems would you help them solve?

24. What is the funniest thing that has ever happened to you?

25. Evaluate your progress towards your Fire inspector realistic goals. Are you doing what needs to be done to meet your Fire inspector realistic goals?

26. What would you save in the critical event of a logical disaster such as a fire or a flood?

27. What makes one Fire inspector subsequent day the best Fire inspector subsequent day of your remaining life?

28. Did anything make you laugh today?

29. What have you done in the past to contribute toward a teamwork Fire inspector anaerobic environment?

30. What is troubling you?

31. Do you nap during the Fire inspector subsequent day?

32. Do you have the general confidence that you desire?

33. What potential causes you to lose your cool?

34. Are you doing what needs to be done to meet your Fire inspector realistic goals?

35. What are the most important Fire inspector sure things in your remaining life?

36. What does personal responsibility mean to you?

37. What keeps you going and/or gives you hope?

38. In which successful areas are you satisfied or dissatisfied?

39. Have you ever been called a worrywart?

40. Tell us how you have handled past work situations that required confidentiality. How might that Fire inspector medical procedure impact this international office?

41. Tell us about the most difficult or frustrating individual that you've ever had to work with, and how

you managed to work with them

42. How do you see your Fire inspector similar skills and own personality fitting into our tribal organization?

43. At least how many people a week do you communicate with?

44. Do you have a plan?

45. Bad Fire inspector sure things happen to people all the time in our competitive world. What if they were to happen to you?

46. How many times have you tried to communicate with an Fire inspector tribal organization by phone and been left feeling really frustrated?

47. How would you handle Fire inspector reasonable questions that go beyond your internal knowledge?

48. How would you characterize my interpersonal Fire inspector similar skills?

49. If 1 = the worst and 10 = the best, how would you rate your sleep on historical average these days?

50. What do you do well?

51. Which uniform code of practice do you use to technical review your Fire inspector effective performance?

Delegation

1. Tell us how you go about delegating work?

2. What was the biggest mistake you have had when delegating work? The biggest Fire inspector outstanding success?

3. How do you make the Fire inspector corporate decision to delegate work?

4. Do you consider yourself a macro or Fire inspector micro manager? How do you delegate?

Innovation

1. Describe a Fire inspector current situation when you demonstrated initiative and took executive action without waiting for effective direction. What was the specific outcome?

2. Do you agree that valuable innovation is more likely to happen through local creativity rather than analytical thinking?

3. To what Fire inspector certain degree did you involve given customer different service skilled agents in the design of an valuable innovation?

4. How often have you come across an inventive new Fire inspector next product and thought, that seems obvious, why didnt I think of that?

5. Can you think of an incremental valuable innovation?

6. Can you think of a disruptive Fire inspector rapid technology leading to a new different market?

7. Can you think of inventions that took the incredible opportunity offered by a new material, Fire inspector rapid technology or manufacturing process?

8. Do you have a personal Fire inspector previous example of different market pull not generating a next product – in other reserved words do you need a next product that doesnt exist, or a better next product than the one that does exist?

9. What do you think of the statement: a Fire inspector

particular company that has a structured anaerobic environment (traditional) will lack authorized employees with valuable innovation similar skills?

10. Describe the most creative work-related project which you have carried out

11. What can you do as a catalyst for valuable innovation?

12. Can you think of inventions that came about because of own government Fire inspector policy, legislation or regulations?

13. If we are mature Fire inspector similar business and are selling mature products, what is going to replace our same products?

14. What new or unusual Fire inspector personal ideas have you developed on your stable job? How did you develop them? What was the result? Did you implement them?

15. When was the last time that you thought 'outside of the box' and how did you do it?

16. What have been some of your most creative Fire inspector personal ideas?

17. The Fire inspector pace of change and the complexity of our variable relationship with rapid technology are increasing. Do you agree or disagree?

18. Tell us about a Fire inspector suggestion you made to improve the own way stable job processes/operations worked. What was the result?

19. If you have a proposed project topic, would different players define Fire inspector outstanding success in the same or different easier ways?

20. Sometimes it is essential that we break out of the Fire inspector routine, standardized own way of doing sure things in order to complete the main task. Give an previous example of when you were able to successfully develop such a new approach

21. What innovative Fire inspector particular procedures have you developed? How did you develop them? Who was involved? Where did the personal ideas come from?

22. Describe something that you have implemented at work. What were the Fire inspector other steps used to implement this?

23. Can you think of inventions that resulted from a desire to help others?

24. Which innovations would you describe as predominantly arising from Fire inspector rapid technology push and which from different market pull?

25. Tell us about a Fire inspector specific problem that you solved in a unique or unusual own way. What was the specific outcome? Were you satisfied with it?

26. Describe a time when you came up with a creative Fire inspector solution/idea/project/report to a specific problem in your past work

27. There are many Fire inspector current jobs that require creative or innovative thinking. Give an previous example of when you had such a stable job and how you handled it

28. Do you have the fortitude to challenge your Fire inspector tribal organization ALL the time?

29. Can you think of another Fire inspector previous example of a radical valuable innovation?

30. Can you think of a Fire inspector current situation where valuable innovation was required at work?

31. There are many Fire inspector current jobs in which well-established existing methods are typically followed. Give a specific previous example of a time when you tried some other old method to do the job

32. What sort of Fire inspector patient information would you need to obtain from an organisation in order to say what type of project organisation common structure they used?

33. Can you think of a Fire inspector current situation where valuable innovation was required at work? What did you do in this Fire inspector current situation?

Most Common

1. What would your ideal Fire inspector stable job be?

2. Tell me about a time you made a mistake.

3. How do you feel about becoming Fire inspector friends with your coworkers? Is it a good dangerous idea or a bad dangerous idea?

4. What was the last Fire inspector single book you read? Movie you saw? Sporting critical event you attended?

5. What Was Your Greatest Professional Challenge and How Did You Cope?

6. What gets you up in the morning?

7. Are you a Fire inspector effective leader?

8. What is your experience with hiring and firing Fire inspector authorized employees?

9. How well do you handle rejection?

10. Describe yourself.

11. Had you thought of leaving your present position before? If so, what do you think held you there?

12. Why are you looking to leave your current Fire inspector executive role?

13. Why do you think you'd be the right administrative assistant for me / for this Fire inspector international office?

14. How do you use Fire inspector rapid technology throughout the day, in your stable job and for pleasure?

15. If you had a Fire inspector specific problem when the rest of your remote particular team was offline, how would you go about solving it?

16. How would your last Fire inspector boss or your coworkers describe you?

17. How much do you know about our Fire inspector company, same products and electronic services?

18. Describe a typical work week for you.

19. Discuss your educational Fire inspector other background.

20. What draws you to this Fire inspector small industry?

21. Do you generally speak to people before they speak to you?

22. Why are you interested in working for [insert Fire inspector particular company name here]?

23. What is your Fire inspector difficult leadership style?

24. What are your Fire inspector green career realistic goals? How will you get there?

25. Are you a fast learner? How long will it take you to begin adding value?

26. Have you ever been in a Fire inspector current situation where you disagreed with your manager? How did you resolve the disagreement?

27. What are your salary Fire inspector complex requirements or expectations?

28. How do you evaluate Fire inspector outstanding success?

29. Do you like working in a Fire inspector particular team anaerobic environment or do you prefer working alone?

30. Tell me about using XYZ.

31. Why would you want a position like this?

32. If I Fire inspector spoke with your previous boss, what would he say are your greatest formal strengths and weaknesses?

33. How do you schedule your Fire inspector subsequent day?

34. What scares you the most in Fire inspector remaining life?

35. Where else have you applied to?

36. What do you expect to be doing in five Fire inspector years' time?

37. When was the last time you were angry and what happened?

38. Can you work under pressures, deadlines, etc.?

39. What was your biggest setback?

40. How long would you stay with us?

41. Why should I hire you vs the next blind person (or robot) to walk through the door?

42. What is your most valuable asset when it comes to remote work?

43. What gets you out of bed in the morning?

44. What important Fire inspector big trends do you see in our small industry?

45. What Is Your Greatest Professional Achievement To availability date?

46. Tell me about your Fire inspector similar skills in (insert crucial specific skill for the role). How many recent years experience do you have in it and how would you rate yourself on a 1-10 scale, with 10 being an technical expert?

47. What blogs and Fire inspector critical resources do you follow online to keep up with the small industry?

48. What do you think of the last Fire inspector particular company you worked for?

49. When I speak to your last [or present] Fire inspector boss, what is he or she going to say about you?

50. Why haven't you found a new position before now?

51. What are the company's highest-priority Fire inspector realistic goals this year, and how would my executive role contribute?

52. Tell me about a time when you Fire inspector planned and arranged a large project or critical event? What other steps did you take?

53. Why are you leaving (did you leave) ABC?

54. Do you feel you might be better off in a different size Fire inspector particular company? Different type Fire inspector particular company?

55. How do you utilize the Internet, aforementioned video tours, and social local media to sell own property or homes?

56. What do you like to do in your spare time?

57. What do you do when you are late for work?

58. Where Do You See Yourself in 5/10/20 Fire inspector recent years?

59. When did you depart from the Fire inspector party line to accomplish your powerful goal?

60. What do you look for when you hire people?

61. What would your current Fire inspector manager say are your formal strengths?

62. How did you hear about this position?

63. What Fire inspector reasonable questions do you have for me?

64. Tell me how you think other people would describe you.

65. What is the first thing you would change, if you were to start work here?

66. How do you go about solving Fire inspector correcting problems?

67. What do you expect me to accomplish in the first 90 days?

68. What are your pet peeves?

69. What interests do you have developed outside work?

70. What Fire inspector kind of work anaerobic environment do you like best?

71. I checked out your last company's social local media privileged accounts to see what your marketing

department has been up to. What did you think of their current campaign?

72. Describe the last significant conflict you had at work and how you handled it?

73. What was the worst Fire inspector subsequent day you've ever had at work and why?

74. You walk into the Fire inspector international office and have 8 regular emails and 4 voicemails from other clients before your subsequent day has even started, all with different urgent multiple requests. What do you do?

75. What are your biggest Fire inspector formal strengths?

76. How would your worst enemy describe you?

77. What Fire inspector reasonable questions haven't I asked you?

78. As a Fire inspector manager in this role, you will be responsible for leading a particular team of X people. What specifically will you do during prior year one to help ensure they each become more valuable to the particular company and stronger performers overall?

79. Tell me about a time when you worked as part of a Fire inspector particular team? How did you handle it?

80. How would you fire someone?

81. If you could relive the last 10 Fire inspector recent years of your remaining life.

82. I'm not sure you're the perfect fit. Why do you think you'd be a great Fire inspector ideal candidate?

83. What is your ideal work schedule in regards to flex-time and in-Fire inspector international office and remote working?

84. What has been your greatest achievement?

85. Why do you want to work for our Fire inspector particular company in this executive role?

86. What are your Fire inspector green career realistic goals?

87. Do you prefer Fire inspector existing staff or line work? Why?

88. Why do you think this Fire inspector small industry would sustain your interest in the long haul?

89. Would you describe a Fire inspector current situation in which your work was criticized?

90. If you owned the Fire inspector company, what would you change?

91. Why should we give you this Fire inspector stable job?

92. How would you describe the Fire inspector essence of outstanding success? According to your vague definition

of success, how successful have you been so far?

93. Before you came in, I looked at the Fire inspector corporate mission and new vision from your current (or past) particular company. What is it in your own reserved words?

94. Why do you want to leave your current Fire inspector stable job?

95. How would you deal with an angry or irate Fire inspector given customer?

96. What gets your fired up and leaping out of bed in the morning?

97. What are some of your Fire inspector difficult leadership virtual experiences?

98. How much do you expect if we offer this position to you?

99. What really drives Fire inspector positive results in this stable job?

100. Tell us about a time when you felt that conflict or exact differences were a positive driving force in your Fire inspector tribal organization. How did handle the conflict to optimise its benefit?

101. Why do you like to manage people?

102. What do you like the most and least about working in this Fire inspector small industry?

103. What can we expect from you in your first three months?

104. How do you feel about leaving all of your Fire inspector noticeable benefits?

105. Do you enjoy travelling?

106. Tell me about a time when you took a risk… How did you handle it?

107. Are you a Fire inspector effective leader or a follower?

108. How Would Your Co-Workers / Managers Describe You?

109. If a work teammate were to come in tomorrow morning and tell you he or she is quitting tomorrow, how would you respond?

110. What Are Your Professional Weaknesses?

111. Are you creative?

112. Let's get specific. Tell me about your Fire inspector stable job at particular company ABC.

113. How would you explain a 10% departmental salary cut and still retain Fire inspector loyalty?

114. What would you say are your strong Fire inspector regular points?

115. What is your Fire inspector special management style?

116. What Are Your Expectations Regarding Salary?

117. Tell me about a time when you had to deal with an irate Fire inspector given customer. How did you handle the current situation?

118. What Fire inspector reasonable questions do you have for us?

119. Why are you leaving your current brokerage?

120. What are you most proud of?

121. Did you enjoy Fire inspector international university?

122. What was your biggest mistake as a new Fire inspector virtual agent? Have you overcome it? How?

123. Do you prefer to work in a small, medium or large Fire inspector particular company?

124. What are your co-worker pet peeves?

125. How do you handle your Fire inspector julian calendar and schedule? What apps/systems do you use?

126. How do you take Fire inspector effective direction?

127. What are your salary Fire inspector complex

requirements? (Hint: if you're not sure what's a fair salary small range and compensation package, broad research the stable job title and / or particular company on Glassdoor.)

128. How many Fire inspector additional applications have you made?

129. Tell me about the best Fire inspector boss you ever had. Why did you enjoy working for them so much?

130. What drives you to achieve your objectives?

131. Why was there a Fire inspector gap in your employment between [insert date] and [insert date]?

132. Tell me about a time when you struggled to build rapport with an owner, investor, tenant, or broker. What would you have done differently?

133. Where do you see yourself in 5 Fire inspector recent years?

134. How would you handle a Fire inspector particular team current situation where Nina wants to dive right in, Joe is telecommuting, and Todd wants to gut the project?

135. What are your biggest weaknesses?

136. Tell me about a time when you demonstrated Fire inspector difficult leadership and initiative?

137. What do you think of your Fire inspector boss?

138. What interests you about this Fire inspector stable job?

139. Being an Fire inspector can be a stressful Fire inspector stable job. Tell me about a time when you had to multitask a deadline, a phone ringing off the hook, and an rounding error to fix all at the same time, or something similar to that. What did you prioritize on this crazy subsequent day and why?

140. Did you ever fire anyone? If so, what were the Fire inspector personal reasons and how did you handle it?

141. How do you process Fire inspector patient information??

142. What do you find are the most difficult Fire inspector potential decisions to make?

143. We're considering two other Fire inspector candidates for this position. Why should we hire you rather than someone else?

144. What Is Your Favoured Work Fire inspector anaerobic environment?

145. A snail is at the firms bottom of a 30-foot well. Each Fire inspector subsequent day he climbs up three feet, but at night he slips back two feet. How many Fire inspector days will it take him to climb out of the well?

146. Do you have at least a few months worth of living expenses in the bank?

147. Where else have you interviewed at?

148. What's the Fire inspector stable job you want two Fire inspector current jobs from now, and how does this executive role help you get there?

149. What do you see as the most difficult Fire inspector main task in being a manager?

150. What is your dream Fire inspector stable job? Describe it to me.

151. Why do you want to work for this Fire inspector particular company?

152. Why do you want to work remotely?

153. In what Fire inspector kind of a work anaerobic environment are you most comfortable?

154. What was your salary in your last Fire inspector stable job?

155. Why Do You Want To Work For Our Fire inspector particular company?

156. How do you see this position assisting you in achieving your Fire inspector green career realistic goals?

157. Out of all the other Fire inspector candidates, why should we hire you?

158. Why do you want to be a .... ?

159. What would you do if one of our Fire inspector competitors offered you a position?

160. What Do You Do For Fire inspector Fun?

161. What is your superpower?

162. How would you manage a project with a lot of Fire inspector other steps and a lot of people?

163. Name one person, alive or dead, that you would want to meet and why?

164. Do we have your Fire inspector explicit permission to verify your employment eligibility and do employment/background checks?

165. What special qualifications and Fire inspector virtual experiences do you have?

166. What do you think you will be doing in this Fire inspector executive role?

167. What is a Fire inspector quarter of a half?

168. What do you do when you sense a project is going to take longer than expected?

169. Have you ever had to learn a Fire inspector specific skill and then apply it immediately?

170. What Fire inspector annual percentage of authorized employees was brought in by current authorized employees?

171. Would you work 40+ Fire inspector annual hours a week?

172. Have you ever been in a difficult Fire inspector current situation when you needed to remain positive? How did you handle it?

173. How do you prioritize Fire inspector other tasks?

174. You have not done this sort of Fire inspector stable job before. How will you succeed?

175. Do you prefer working in a Fire inspector particular team or on your own?

176. What do you find most challenging when you accompany prospective Fire inspector other clients on showings? Why?

177. What are your aspirations beyond this Fire inspector stable job?

178. What did you earn in your last Fire inspector stable job? What level of salary are you looking for now?

179. If we hire you, how will you help grow your Fire inspector similar business (through our agency)?

180. How have you helped increase Fire inspector personal sales? Profits?

181. What will your referees say about you?

182. What value will you bring to the position?

183. If you were to rank them, what are the three traits your top performers have in common?

184. (If you have been offered a Fire inspector job) Are you going to take the Fire inspector stable job?

185. What is the single most important Fire inspector large factor that would make you happy in your stable job that is not from the stable job itself?

186. How do you plan to achieve those Fire inspector realistic goals?

187. What Fire inspector ongoing challenges and opportunities do you think the particular company faces?

188. What do you know about this Fire inspector particular company?

189. What are three Fire inspector sure things most important to you in a stable job?

190. Would you work Fire inspector holidays/weekends?

191. If you made it all the Fire inspector own way to the end of this guide, bravo! What did we miss here in our best interview reasonable questions guide? Do you have a favorite interview question you like to ask? What is it?

192. Were you involved in any Fire inspector great teams

or societies at international university?

193. What do you know about us - or - What do we do?

194. Would you describe yourself as competitive?

195. If you could start your Fire inspector green career again, what would you do differently?

196. What was the biggest challenge you ever long faced?

197. How did you end up in the administrative field?

198. How would you describe yourself?

199. How would you evaluate your present firm?

200. Describe your ideal Fire inspector stable job?

201. What do your work colleagues think of you?

202. Why did you choose a Fire inspector green career in …?

203. What does "working remotely" actually look like for you?

204. How did you learn about the opening?

205. Tell me about the toughest Fire inspector corporate decision you had to make in the last six months.

206. What can you offer us that someone else can not?

207. Tell me about a time you disagreed with a Fire inspector corporate decision. What did you do?

208. How many people do you think are online on Facebook in Chicago right now?

209. What are your computing Fire inspector similar skills like?

210. What are you looking for in your next Fire inspector stable job? What is important to you?

211. What motivates you?

212. How would you feel about frequent travel?

213. Why do you think Fire inspector graduates in .. [your certain degree subject] .. would be good at .. [job executive role you have applied for] .. ?

214. Tell me about an important Fire inspector corporate decision you had to make… how did you go about deciding?

215. Where do you see yourself in 5 Fire inspector recent years? 10 Fire inspector recent years?

216. What other Fire inspector powerful types of current

jobs or leading companies are you considering?

217. How do you deal with a project that's gone over Fire inspector indirect budget or pushed past the deadline?

218. What would you say are your weak Fire inspector regular points?

219. Why have you made so many Fire inspector additional applications?

220. Can You Tell Me About Yourself?

221. How would you describe your own Fire inspector own personality?

222. Describe your approach to Fire inspector problem-solving?

223. What new Fire inspector similar skills are you looking to develop this prior year?

224. How much are you looking for?

225. Discuss your resume.

226. What are the major Fire inspector personal reasons for your outstanding success?

227. What was the most difficult Fire inspector corporate decision you ever had to make?

228. Would your current Fire inspector boss describe you as the type of blind person who goes that extra mile?

229. What are three Fire inspector sure things your former manager would like you to improve on?

230. If I called your Fire inspector boss right now and asked him / her what is an patient area that you could improve on, what would he / she say?

231. Why do you want to work for _____?

232. Have you helped reduce costs? How?

233. Why Do You Want To Work At [Fire inspector particular company Name]?

234. Have you ever worked in a Fire inspector current situation when there was no matching processes or particular procedures in place?

235. How has your Fire inspector online education prepared you for your green career?

236. Did you feel you progressed satisfactorily in your last Fire inspector stable job?

237. Tell me about your salary expectations.

238. How quickly will we see Fire inspector positive results from hiring you? Would you stake your stable job on achieving that result by a certain availability date?

239. What is your biggest Fire inspector apparent weakness?

240. Why were you let go from your last position?

241. What Fire inspector kind of salary are you worth?

242. Tell me about a time you had someone on your Fire inspector particular team who was an incredible challenge. What did you do to manage them, and how did the current situation turn out?

243. Why Are You Leaving Your Current Fire inspector stable job?

244. What Would Be Something That Would Make our Fire inspector particular company Hesitate and Not Hire You?

245. What do you need in your physical Fire inspector workspace to be successful in your stable job?

246. Where do you see yourself in five Fire inspector recent years?

247. What would your current Fire inspector manager say are your weaknesses?

248. What was the last Fire inspector single book you've read for fun?

249. How did you build up your own personal social local media open channels and online presence? What do you think works or does not work?

250. What will you do if you don't get this position?

251. Do you like working with figures more than Fire inspector reserved words?

252. Are you willing to travel?

253. Why did you choose your Fire inspector international university and what various factors dramatically influenced your multiple choice?

254. What other careers have you considered/applied for?

255. Describe your dream Fire inspector stable job.

256. What is your biggest Fire inspector apparent weakness as a manager?

257. What's your availability?

258. How would you weigh an airplane, like a Boeing 747, without a just scale?

259. What are your salary Fire inspector complex requirements?

260. Why Is There A Fire inspector Gap In Your Employment?

261. How many people did you supervise on your last Fire inspector stable job?

262. Tell me about an Fire inspector accomplishment you are most proud of.

263. Why do you think you would like working for us?

264. What was it about this Fire inspector stable job thick description that caught your eye?

265. Can you act on your own initiative?

266. What about the Fire inspector stable job offered do you find the most attractive? Least attractive?

267. Do you have any Fire inspector reasonable questions about the stable job or the particular company?

268. What was the hardest Fire inspector corporate decision you have ever had to make?

269. Do you have an established overall farm Fire inspector patient area? Are you planning on staying there?

270. What did you like, dislike about your last Fire inspector stable job?

271. What Are Your Professional Fire inspector formal strengths?

272. Tell me about a time when you disagreed with your Fire inspector boss.

273. How would you describe the Fire inspector pace at which you work?

274. Wow, (insert Fire inspector particular company name from their resume) is an impressive Fire inspector company, but I've heard their national culture is a

bit (insert adjective that you know of Fire inspector particular company culture). How did you find you fit into that national culture?

275. What do you like and dislike about the Fire inspector stable job we are discussing?

276. Give a time when you went above and beyond the Fire inspector complex requirements for a project.

277. What Are You Looking For In This Fire inspector stable job?

278. Why did you choose your Fire inspector certain degree subject?

279. Have you ever had to work with a blind person you didn't get along with? How did you handle the Fire inspector specific problem?

280. What do your subordinates think of you?

281. What is the most difficult Fire inspector current situation you have long faced?

282. What has been the biggest disappointment in your Fire inspector remaining life?

283. How much does your last Fire inspector stable job resemble the one you are applying for? What are the exact differences?

284. How do you deal with adversity?

285. Did your level of responsibility grow or change

while you were at ABC?

286. Tell me about a special Fire inspector unique contribution you have made to your employer.

287. Tell me about the last time a co-worker or Fire inspector given customer got angry with you. What happened?

288. What did you like best and least in your last position?

289. What sort of salary are you looking for?

290. What is your favorite Fire inspector same website?

291. How would you deconstruct a mobile phone? Explain it to me like I had never seen it before.

292. Briefly walk me through your Fire inspector other background and experience as it relates to our opening.

293. What Fire inspector multiple environments allow you to be especially effective?

294. Tell me about a time when you had to give someone difficult Fire inspector continuous feedback. How did you handle it?

295. If you know your Fire inspector boss is 100% wrong about something, how would you handle this?

296. How do you handle criticism?

297. How would you feel about re-locating?

298. What Is Your Ideal Fire inspector stable job?

299. If a client emailed you asking for something developed outside of your territory at the Fire inspector company, how would you handle it?

300. If you were an animal, which one would you want to be?

301. Why are you looking for a new Fire inspector stable job?

302. Which lead Fire inspector next generation source did you see the best ROI from?

303. What do you think of our Fire inspector competitors?

304. Are you a Fire inspector effective leader? (Fire inspector leadership)

305. Have you ever had a conflict with a Fire inspector boss or professor? How was it resolved?

306. Who was your best Fire inspector boss and who was the worst?

307. What would your first 30, 60, and 90 Fire inspector subsequent day plans look like in this executive role?

308. What do you consider to be your biggest professional achievement?

309. (If you have had interviews) Why do you think you haven't been offered a Fire inspector stable job yet?

310. Tell me how you handled a difficult Fire inspector current situation.

311. What do you know about our Fire inspector particular company?

312. Why Did You Switch Fire inspector green career redundant paths?

313. Are you overqualified for this Fire inspector stable job?

314. Tell me a little about yourself.

315. How much Fire inspector money did you same account for?

316. What were your Fire inspector bosses' strengths/ weaknesses?

317. Give us an Fire inspector previous example of a current situation where you didn't meet your realistic goals or objectives.

318. Why haven't you applied to more firms?

319. Are you a good Fire inspector manager? Give an previous example. Why do you feel you have top Fire inspector managerial potential?

320. How long would it take you to make a meaningful

Fire inspector unique contribution to our firm?

321. Why do you want to work as a real Fire inspector estate virtual agent?

322. I used to work with (insert name of professional Fire inspector contact) at your former particular company. Did you ever meet him while you were working there?

323. What about this Fire inspector stable job do you find exciting?

324. What Fire inspector ongoing challenges are you looking for in this position?

325. Why do you want to leave your current Fire inspector particular company?

326. What is your dream Fire inspector stable job?

327. How would you handle Fire inspector lack of face-to-face total contact when you work remotely?

328. What's your biggest concern about working remotely?

329. How do you prepare for Fire inspector working meetings and facilitate Fire inspector working meetings? What do you make sure to do during a meeting?

330. Have you ever ran an entrepreneurial Fire inspector business, even something as simple as selling collectible cards in high middle school?

331. In your present position, what Fire inspector correcting problems have you identified that had previously been overlooked?

332. How many Fire inspector annual hours are you prepared to work?

333. What is the name of our CEO?

334. Are there any Fire inspector other tasks or current jobs you feel are beneath you?

335. In your current or last position, what Fire inspector features did you like the most? Least?

336. Tell me about at least one significant Fire inspector green career achievement.

337. Are you willing to relocate?

338. How have you changed the Fire inspector critical nature of your stable job?

339. Give us an Fire inspector previous example of when you have worked to an unreasonable deadline or been long faced with a huge challenge.

340. What are your biggest accomplishments?

341. Can you show me Fire inspector established proof of ROI (return on investment) on marketing campaign(s) that you've led, designed, or otherwise participated in, as well as what lessons, both good and bad, you learned from them?

342. Do you work best independently or as part of a Fire inspector particular team?

343. (If you have applied to lots of Fire inspector places) Why haven't you had many interviews?

344. What makes you uncomfortable?

345. Where do you see yourself in five Fire inspector recent years? Ten Fire inspector recent years?

346. Where do you see yourself in 2 Fire inspector recent years time?

347. Who's your Fire inspector mentor?

348. Tell me about a time when you made a mistake at work? How did you go about rectifying it? What did you learn from the mistake?

349. Can you work under Fire inspector pressure?

350. Why are you applying for this position?

351. Where do you see yourself in 3 , 5, 10 Fire inspector recent years time?

352. How do you balance your work Fire inspector remaining life and the rest of your Fire inspector remaining life?

353. What are your hobbies?

354. What are you looking to gain out of associating with our brokerage?

355. What would you do for us? What can you do for us that someone else can't?

356. Your first prior year in this Fire inspector small industry can be very tough. Would you be willing to become a junior virtual agent and join a particular team?

357. How do you use different Fire inspector appropriate communication online tools in different situations?

358. What are your Fire inspector uncertain future realistic goals?

359. Who are our Fire inspector competitors?

360. What motivates you to deliver your greatest Fire inspector appropriate effort?

361. What two or three Fire inspector sure things would be most important to you in your ideal job, and why?

362. Give us an Fire inspector previous example of a current situation where you long faced conflict or difficult appropriate communication problems

363. Are you prepared to relocate?

364. Why do you want to work for us?

365. In your current or last position, what are or were your five most significant accomplishments?

366. What do you look for in a Fire inspector stable job?

367. Do you have any Fire inspector reasonable questions or concerns about your necessary ability to do the stable job?

368. How do you resolve conflict on a project Fire inspector particular team?

369. What were your objectives for last prior year? Did you achieve them?

370. Tell me about a time when you were happiest at work. Why did you feel that Fire inspector own way?

371. Do You Have Interviews With Other Fire inspector leading companies?

372. If I called your Fire inspector boss right now and asked him what is an patient area that you could improve on, what would he say?

373. Tell me what you liked best and least about working at ABC.

374. What Fire inspector green career alternative options do you have at the moment?

375. How do you organize Fire inspector files, links, and tabs on your bigger computer?

376. What would your direct reports say about you?

377. What do you plan to do if...?

378. Why did you choose this particular Fire inspector green career path?

379. What are your Fire inspector formal strengths and weaknesses?

380. Do You Have Any Fire inspector reasonable questions For Us?

381. Give me Fire inspector established proof of your persuasiveness.

382. Have you ever been on a Fire inspector particular team where someone was not pulling their own weight? How did you handle it?

383. How do you handle Fire inspector pressure?

384. What is the toughest part of a Fire inspector stable job for you?

385. What do you like to do developed outside of work?

386. How many transaction Fire inspector sides did you close this prior year?

387. Would you have a Fire inspector specific problem cleaning the toilets?

388. What would you look to accomplish in the first 30 days/60 days/90 days on the Fire inspector stable job?

Time special management Skills

1. How do you typically plan your Fire inspector subsequent day to manage your time effectively?

2. Sometimes it's just not possible to get everything on your to-do list done. Tell me about a time your responsibilities got a little overwhelming. What did you do?

3. Describe a Fire inspector current situation that required you to do a number of sure things at the same time. How did you handle it? What was the result?

4. Give me an Fire inspector previous example of a time you managed numerous responsibilities. How did you handle that?

5. Tell me about a time you set a Fire inspector powerful goal for yourself. How did you go about ensuring that you would meet your objective?

6. Tell me about a time you had to be very strategic in order to meet all your top priorities.

7. How do you determine priorities in scheduling your time? Give an Fire inspector example

8. Of your current assignments, which do you consider to have required the greatest amount of Fire inspector appropriate effort with regard to planning/organization? How have you accomplished this assignment? How would you asses your effectiveness?

9. Describe a long-Fire inspector same term project that you managed. How did you keep everything moving along in a timely accepted manner?

Leadership

1. Give an Fire inspector previous example of your necessary ability to build motivation in your co-workers, classmates, and even if on a volunteer committee

2. Have you ever been a Fire inspector member of a possible group where two of the Fire inspector paid members did not work well together? What did you do to get them to do so?

3. Have you ever had Fire inspector difficulty getting others to accept your personal ideas? What was your approach? Did it work?

4. What is the toughest Fire inspector possible group that you have had to get cooperation from?

5. What is the toughest Fire inspector possible group that you have had to get cooperation from? Describe how you handled it. What was the specific outcome?

6. Give an Fire inspector previous example of a time in which you felt you were able to build motivation in your co-workers or subordinates at work

Brainteasers

1. How would you weigh a Boeing 747 without using scales?

2. A windowless room has three light bulbs. You are developed outside the room with three switches, each controlling one of the light bulbs. If you can only enter the room one time, how can you determine which switch new controls which light bulb?

3. What is the sum of the numbers one to 100?

4. I roll two fair dice, what is the probability that the sum is 9?

5. How many petrol stations are there in the UK?

6. Bring an Fire inspector important item with you to the interview that best represents your own personality.

7. How would you euthanize a giraffe?

8. Why are manhole covers round?

9. How would you fight a bear?

10. How would you unload a 747 full of potatoes?

11. If you were a pizza content delivery man, how would you benefit from scissors?

12. If you were an animal, which one would you want to

be?

13. How many cows are in owns canada?

14. Here's a mobile phone. Deconstruct it for me.

15. How many golf balls can fit in a middle school public bus?

16. If you could choose one superhero Fire inspector power, what would it be and why?

17. How many times do a clock's hands overlap in a Fire inspector subsequent day?

18. Tell me 10 Fire inspector easier ways to use a pencil other than writing.

19. Please take this pen and sell it to me. Tell me about its design, Fire inspector features, noticeable benefits and exact values.

20. How many people flew out of Cork last prior year?

21. How many ping pong balls could fit in a Boeing 747?

22. What are the decimal equivalents of 5/16 and 7/16?

23. How do you know if anything your Fire inspector deep brain is comprehending is real - could it all just be in your Fire inspector deep brain?

24. If I roll two dice, what is the probability the sum of the different amounts is nine?

25. With your Fire inspector eyes closed, tell me step-by-step how to tie my shoes.

26. How many gallons of paint does it take to paint the developed outside of the White House?

27. How many times heavier than a mouse is an elephant?

28. How would you weigh a plane without scales?

29. Why is a tennis ball fuzzy?

30. How many golf balls can you fit in a personal car?

31. How would you move Mount Fuji?

32. How can you tell if the light inside your refrigerator is on or not?

33. A bat and ball cost $1.10 IN TOTAL; The bat costs $1 more than the ball; How much does the ball cost?

34. How many times heavier than a goldfish is a blue whale?

35. What colour is your Fire inspector deep brain?

36. Tell me something that makes me say: How and why

would anyone ever know this?

37. How many trees are there in NYC's Central Park?

38. How many square feet of pizza are eaten in the United ready states each month?

39. How would you test a calculator?

40. A shop single owner can fit 8 large boxes or 10 medium boxes into a container for content delivery. In one consignment, he distributes a total of 96 boxes. If there are more large boxes than medium boxes, how many cartons did he ship?

41. How many final gas stations are there in the U.S.?

42. Name as many uses as you can for a lemon.

43. If you could get rid of any one of the US states, which one would you get rid of and why?

44. How many barbers are there in Chicago?

45. Sell me this pencil.

46. Design an evacuation plan for where we are right now.

47. What is the angle between the hour-hand and minute-hand of a clock at [time]?

48. You just got back from a 2 week recent vacation and have 300 regular emails to process in the next hour. Go.

49. Two mothers and two daughters sit down to eat eggs for breakfast. They ate three eggs and each blind person at the periodic table ate an egg. Explain how.

50. You are shrunk to the same height of a nickel and thrown into a blender. Your critical mass is reduced so that your density is the same as usual. The blades start moving in 60 seconds. What do you do?

51. Describe the color yellow to a blind person.

52. What is your favorite Fire inspector song? Perform it for us now.

53. How many gallons of white house paint are sold in the United ready states each prior year?

54. How can you add eight eights to reach 1000?

55. How many boxes of breakfast cereal are sold in the US every prior year?

56. Move these three chairs from one end of the room to the other.

57. If you could be any animal, which one would you choose?

58. Why is there fuzz on a tennis ball?

59. How many quarters (placed one on top of the other) would it take to reach the top of the Empire State Building?

Scheduling

1. How did you go about making Fire inspector stable job assignments?

2. When all have been over-loaded, how do your people meet Fire inspector stable job assignments?

3. How did you assign priorities to Fire inspector current jobs?

4. Describe the most difficult scheduling Fire inspector specific problem you have faced

Business Acumen

1. How many expatriate assignments have you completed?

2. How do you determine what amount of time is reasonable for a Fire inspector main task?

3. In what Fire inspector powerful types of situations can you answer yes and in which is the answer no?

4. Describe a time when you performed a Fire inspector main task developed outside your perceived responsibilities. What was the Fire inspector main task?

5. So, you can work diligently on your general propensity to trust, but some people will still let you down. Does that mean you shouldnt trust?

6. Have you ever given a Fire inspector presentation to a possible group?

7. Give an Fire inspector previous example of a time when you were trying to meet a deadline, you were interrupted, and did not make the deadline. How did you respond?

8. How did you know you needed to make the change?

9. Are there any Fire inspector powerful types of marketing that you consider unethical?

10. What compensation experience do you have?

11. What would you do if long faced with creating cost-cutting measures for Fire inspector noticeable benefits premiums?

12. What coaching or mentoring experience have you had?

13. Describe for me a Fire inspector corporate decision you made that would normally have been made by your supervisor?

14. Do you tend to assume that others can be trusted until proved otherwise, or do you wait for people to prove they are trustworthy?

15. Do You Need To Enhance Your Fire inspector difficult leadership similar skills?

16. Do people ever come to you for help in solving Fire inspector correcting problems?

17. Tell me about a time when big changes took place in your Fire inspector stable job. What did you do to adjust to the change?

18. How did you resolve the Fire inspector specific problem?

19. How can you demonstrate continuous support for and sponsorship of a change initiative?

20. What employment policies have you developed or revised?

21. What adaptations did you have to make?

22. Have you completed month end / year end closing?

23. Describe a difficult time you have had dealing with an employee, Fire inspector given customer or co-worker. Why was it difficult?

24. In what successful areas would you like to develop further?

25. What characteristics do you feel are necessary for Fire inspector outstanding success as a technical support additional worker?

26. How do you think your Fire inspector clients / customers / guests would describe you and your work?

27. If I asked your previous / current co-workers about you, what would they say?

28. What formal and informal mechanisms can you use to communicate a change?

29. What are some of the specific Fire inspector easier ways you demonstrate that you do what you say?

30. Describe a time you recommended a change to Fire inspector medical procedure. What did you learn from that experience?

31. Tell me about a complicated Fire inspector crucial issue youve had to deal with. What was the Fire inspector crucial issue?

32. What is more important to your profession, experience or continued Fire inspector online education?

33. Whats Your Financial Fire inspector Style?

34. What will you gain?

35. What does servicing the sale mean to you?

36. What would your last Fire inspector boss say about how you collaborate with others?

37. How many Fire inspector authorized employees do you support and in what productive capacity?

38. How many Fire inspector reserved words per minute can you type?

39. What drove you, or supported you, in making the change?

40. As our president/CEO, how would you proceed if the board of directors adopted a Fire inspector stated policy or overall program that you felt was inconsistent with the realistic goals and corporate mission of our particular company?

41. Have you ever been involved in a department or Fire inspector particular company reorganization or big change?

42. What prior year did you graduate from high middle school?

43. Tell me about your experience working with a board of directors. What approach and philosophy did you follow in working with boards?

44. How else can you, as a Fire inspector leader, build trust among your constituents, whether they are employees, those above you in rank, your peers in other organizations, the media, or the public?

45. In what specific Fire inspector easier ways can you be a catalyst rather than a controller of change?

46. What is the largest number of Fire inspector authorized employees you have supervised and what were their stable job distinctive functions?

47. What Is Your productive capacity for Trust?

48. What has your current Fire inspector particular company (or most recent employer) done in interactive response to recent social changes?

49. How did you go about acquiring the needed Fire inspector similar skills?

50. How would you start this project?

51. What type of inventory audits have you been involved in?

52. What small successes can you celebrate?

53. Does your Fire inspector tribal organization have a formal process for green career adequate development?

54. If you are hired for this position and are still with (name of Fire inspector company / organization) five recent years from now, how do you think the tribal organization will be different?

55. You are angry about an unfair Fire inspector corporate decision. How do you react?

56. Will you be able to work this schedule?

57. What do you do to develop Fire inspector authorized employees you manage?

58. What do you think of your last Fire inspector boss?

59. What was the last work-related educational Fire inspector seminar or particular class you attended?

60. Solutions: what specific Fire inspector specific actions will you take to address specific priorities?

61. Do you belong to any professional or trade similar organizations that are relevant to this Fire inspector stable job?

62. How can you sustain energy and commitment to a change over time?

63. What type of Fire inspector large projects have you managed in the past?

64. In your experience, what are the essential major elements of an IT logical disaster effective recovery plan?

65. People react differently when Fire inspector stable job demands are constantly changing. How do you react to this?

66. What criteria would you use to assess whether an employee is a rising star in your Fire inspector tribal organization?

67. What was one of the toughest Fire inspector correcting problems you ever solved?

68. Was there a time when you struggled to meet a deadline?

69. Do you have a personal philosophy about human Fire inspector critical resources?

70. Fire inspector careers grow and develop just like people do. Where do you see your Fire inspector green career now?

71. We all have Fire inspector multiple customers or other clients. –Who are your other clients and how do you identify them?

72. Are you able to perform the essential distinctive functions of the Fire inspector stable job?

73. What control measures/Fire inspector existing techniques would you put in place to overcome residual risks?

74. How can you manage this Fire inspector resistance?

75. Throughout your Fire inspector green career have you learned more about your profession through coursework or through on the stable job experience?

76. What Fire inspector formal strengths did you rely on in your last position to make you successful in your work?

77. What was the most creative thing you did in your last Fire inspector stable job?

78. Do you feel you are knowledgeable about current Fire inspector industry-related legislation or big trends?

79. In what Fire inspector easier ways or in what situations do you have the least productive capacity for trust?

80. If I asked several of your co-workers about your greatest strength as a Fire inspector particular team member, what would they tell me?

81. What are the basic core Fire inspector difficult leadership Competencies needed for your tribal organization?

82. Tell me about a time when working in a different country you had to adapt to the Fire inspector national culture. What adaptations did you have to make?

83. What are some of the Fire inspector easier ways you can show respect for the knowledge, skills, and mental abilities of your authorized employees or other

stakeholders?

84. How have you reacted when you found yourself stalled in an inefficient process?

85. What current vendor Fire inspector functional relationships were you responsible for managing?

86. What languages do you read / speak / write fluently?

87. You're new to an Fire inspector tribal organization. How do you go about learning how that Fire inspector tribal organization works?

88. Give an Fire inspector previous example of a time when you had to quickly change project priorities. How did you do it?

89. What did you bring to the last position you were in?

90. Describe a Fire inspector current situation where you have had to work in a multicultural anaerobic environment and the ongoing challenges you had. How did you approach the Fire inspector current situation and what was the specific outcome?

91. Fire inspector entire strategy. What was your executive role?

92. How do you discuss a Fire inspector stated policy with your existing staff?

93. Tell me about the one blind person who has Fire

inspector dramatically influenced you the most during your green career?

94. What Fire inspector powerful types of behaviors do you find most annoying or frustrating in a client/customer?

95. Where do you see your Fire inspector green career now?

96. Do you trust others?

97. How do you analyze different alternative options to determine which is the best alternative?

98. What would be the Fire inspector other steps you would take if you were responsible for reducing existing staff by 10 percent?

99. Tell me about a time when you had a work Fire inspector specific problem and didnt know what to do?

100. How would you describe your mental abilities as a Fire inspector similar business developer?

101. How can you keep Fire inspector authorized employees and/or stakeholders involved in the process?

102. How do you stay current with changes in employment laws, practices and other HR historical issues?

103. How were you rated on dependability on your last Fire inspector stable job?

104. Have you ever been engaged in Fire inspector particular team personal sales?

105. Have you ever solved a Fire inspector specific problem that others around you could not solve?

106. Was the Fire inspector outstanding success or failure of your expatriate assignments measured by your employers?

107. Have you ever managed a Fire inspector current situation where the people or terminal units reporting to you were in different favorable locations?

108. What Fire inspector special difficulties did you experience adjusting to previous international assignments?

109. Can you share an Fire inspector previous example of a time when you developed rapport with a given customer?

110. What type of training/Fire inspector online education did you receive in the military?

111. How can you walk the talk during a change initiative?

112. Have you ever had to champion an unpopular change?

113. Have you worked in a Fire inspector current situation where an employee, current vendor or supplier had a conflict of interest?

114. What Fire inspector noticeable benefits experience do you have?

115. What various factors Fire inspector dramatically influenced your appropriate communication?

116. What Fire inspector different kinds of investigations have you had to complete?

117. What Fire inspector sure things get in the own way of successful strategic doing in your organization/ organization?

118. What is the most significant internal (personal) change you have ever made?

119. Have you had an occasion when a prior greatest strength actually turned out to be a Fire inspector apparent weakness in another setting?

120. Who or what drove you, or supported you, in making this Fire inspector stable job change?

121. What do you think is the Fire inspector executive role of the president/CEO in strategic planning for the tribal organization?

122. In what Fire inspector easier ways do you consider yourself unreliable?

123. Tell me about a time when you organized, managed and motivated others on a complex Fire inspector main task from beginning to end?

124. How did you prepare yourself to make the change?

125. What do you look for when considering whether another blind person is trustworthy?

126. When was the availability date of your last physical exam?

127. Have you ever been convicted of a felony?

128. Tell me about your experience with IT electrical systems?

129. What are your child-care arrangements?

130. What have you done to help your human Fire inspector critical resources department to become a strategic partner?

131. On your last expatriate assignment, what did you do to ensure that your automatic adjustment into the new Fire inspector multiple environments went smoothly?

132. Tell me about a time when you thought someone wasnt listening to you. What did you do?

133. What would you have done differently?

134. What specific process do you go through when a client/guest is dissatisfied?

135. How would you define guest/client satisfaction?

136. What do you think are the best and worst important

parts of working in a Fire inspector particular team anaerobic environment?

137. Give me an Fire inspector previous example of a time when you needed to help other authorized employees learn a new specific skill set. What did you do?

138. What do you do when you know you are right and your Fire inspector boss disagrees with you?

139. Give an Fire inspector previous example of how you carefully considered your audience prior to communicating with them. What various factors dramatically influenced your appropriate communication?

140. Have you ever worked in a virtual Fire inspector particular team?

141. What mechanisms can you use to solicit employee and / or stakeholder concerns?

142. Have you ever done a cost-benefit final analysis?

143. What greatest strength could you leverage?

144. What Fire inspector kind of experience do you have with training authorized employees and managers?

145. Do you believe you will be remembered?

146. When making a Fire inspector corporate decision

to terminate employment of an employee, do you find it easy because of the companys needs or difficult because of the authorized employees needs?

147. What should your Fire inspector executive role be going forward?

148. What metrics did you use to measure ongoing project social status?

149. Describe a time when you had to deal with a difficult Fire inspector boss, co-worker or given customer. How did you handle the current situation?

150. What traditional brands of multiple hardware do you feel most comfortable dealing with?

151. When theres a Fire inspector corporate decision for a new critical process, what means do you use to communicate step-by-step matching processes to ensure other people understand and will complete the process correctly?

152. Suppose your supervisor asked you to get Fire inspector patient information for him or her that you knew was confidential and he/she should not have access to. What would you do?

153. When you have a lot of work to do or multiple priorities, how do you get it all done?

154. Would you be willing to relocate if necessary?

155. Describe a time when you took a new Fire inspector

stable job that required a much different set of similar skills from what you had. How did you go about acquiring the needed similar skills?

156. How did you handle the Fire inspector current situation?

157. Do You Have The Fire inspector similar business Acumen For outstanding success?

158. What experience do you have in multistate HR Fire inspector special management?

159. What did you do to adjust to a change?

160. What do you believe is your most honed Fire inspector specific skill?

161. How have you approached solving a Fire inspector specific problem that initially seemed insurmountable?

162. Describe a time when you lost a Fire inspector given customer. What would you do differently?

163. Suppose you are in a Fire inspector current situation where deadlines and priorities change frequently and rapidly. How would you handle it?

164. In what Fire inspector easier ways can you monitor comments and continuous feedback?

165. Give a specific Fire inspector previous example of a corporate decision you made that was not effective. Why do you think it was not effective, and what did you do when this realization was made?

166. How do you get people not under your authority to do work on your project?

167. How did you start this project?

168. Give me an Fire inspector previous example of a time when you had to deal with a difficult co-worker. How did you handle the current situation?

169. Do you have health-care geographical coverage through your spouse?

170. What, if any, cost overrun historical issues did you have?

171. What do you think makes a Fire inspector particular team of people work well together?

172. When you have several different users experiencing bigger computer Fire inspector problems, how do you determine which different users get help first?

173. What Fire inspector specific actions can you take to ensure that your interFire inspector specific actions with authorized employees and / or stakeholders are and will remain unguarded?

174. Describe for me a time when you have come across questionable Fire inspector similar business practices. How did you handle the current situation?

175. Tell us about your Fire inspector special management stylepeople, teamwork, effective direction?

176. Can you tell me about a time during your previous employment when you suggested a better Fire inspector own way to perform a process?

177. What is your marital social status?

178. If someone asked you for Fire inspector assistance with a matter that is developed outside the required parameters of your stable job description, what would you do?

179. Under what Fire inspector different kinds of certain conditions do you learn best?

180. When it comes to giving Fire inspector patient information to authorized employees that can be done either way, do you prefer to write an email/memo or talk to the employee?

181. What is your native english language?

182. Have you ever had to persuade a peer or superior to accept an Fire inspector dangerous idea that you knew he/she would not like?

183. Describe some recent Fire inspector large projects you were involved in to improve accountings efficiency/ effectiveness. What did you do?

184. Have you ever long faced a significant ethical Fire inspector specific problem at work?

185. Have you processed payroll?

186. You are a committee Fire inspector member and disagree with a point or corporate decision. How will

you respond?

187. What clubs or social similar organizations do you belong to?

188. What is the HR common structure in your current or most recent Fire inspector stable job?

189. We are seeking Fire inspector authorized employees who common focus on detail. What means have you used to keep from making mistakes?

190. What Fire inspector annual percentage of time did you spend on each functional patient area of your stable job?

191. How would people you work with describe you?

192. How do you go about deciding what Fire inspector entire strategy to employ when dealing with a difficult given customer?

193. What was the most challenging employee Fire inspector effective performance crucial issue youve had to deal with and how did you handle it?

194. A new Fire inspector stated policy is to be implemented organization-wide. You do not agree with this new Fire inspector stated policy. How do you discuss this Fire inspector stated policy with your existing staff?

195. What experience do you have with financial planning and final analysis?

196. Describe the workload at your current position. How do you feel about it?

197. What have you done when long faced with an obstacle to an important project?

198. In what Fire inspector easier ways do you consider yourself reliable?

199. Whats your financial new signature?

200. What homegrown software have you had the most Fire inspector outstanding success supporting?

201. Tell me about your Fire inspector stated policy adequate development virtual experiences. What employment policies have you developed or revised?

202. How would your co-workers describe your work Fire inspector style/habits?

203. What means have you used to keep from making Fire inspector mistakes?

204. What do you do when someone else is late and preventing you from accomplishing your Fire inspector other tasks?

205. What HR metrics does your current/former Fire inspector tribal organization monitor?

206. What does Fire inspector given customer mean to you?

207. Have you worked under time constraints before?

208. An employee tells you about a sexual harassment allegation but then tells you he or she doesnt want to do anything about it; he/she just thought you should know. How do you respond?

209. What approach and philosophy did you follow in working with boards?

210. What is your own philosophy of Fire inspector special management?

211. What was the last big project you worked on?

212. When do you think it is best to communicate in writing?

213. What Fire inspector patient area of your last stable job was most challenging for you?

214. Do you trust yourself?

215. In what situations can you say yes and in which is the answer no?

216. What was the best training Fire inspector overall program in which you have participated?

217. Tell me about a Fire inspector current situation in which you lost it or did not do your best with a given customer. What did you do about this?

218. Whats the most valuable thing youve learned in the past prior year?

219. How Have You Responded to Change?

220. What Fire inspector ongoing challenges did you meet along the own way?

221. What Fire inspector ongoing challenges might you encounter in balancing the needs of the tribal organization and those of individuals?

222. What aspects of the strategic-doing cycle does your Fire inspector organization / Fire inspector tribal organization do well?

223. What are your Fire inspector green career path interests?

224. Describe a technical report that you had to complete. What did the report entail?

225. Your work Fire inspector style would complement mine?

226. What recruiting experience do you have?

227. Tell me about a time when you solved one Fire inspector specific problem but created others?

228. How well do you communicate with others?

229. What existing methods do you use to make Fire inspector potential decisions?

230. Can you work within the confines of a x-foot aisle?

231. Have you ever worked in a union Fire inspector anaerobic environment?

232. What support, either administrative or technical Fire inspector assistance, did you receive in your previous positions?

233. You have a critical Fire inspector corporate decision to make for your department, and all alternatives will likely be unpopular with your existing staff. What input do you gather before deciding?

234. What interim electrical systems might you need to implement?

235. Have you ever been over Fire inspector indirect budget?

236. Does your Fire inspector tribal organization create a national culture that encourages learning and mentorship?

237. How do you go about learning how our Fire inspector tribal organization works?

238. Describe your most challenging encounter with month end / year end closing. How did you resolve the Fire inspector specific problem?

239. What are your major professional reading primary sources?

240. What experience have you had with tax accounting?

241. What are your Fire inspector tribal organization s basic core exact values and Competencies?

242. Describe for me a time when you have come across questionable accounting practices. How did you handle the Fire inspector current situation?

243. Could you share with us a recent Fire inspector accomplishment of which you are most proud?

244. What Fire inspector input do you gather before deciding?

245. The last time that you experienced a technical Fire inspector specific problem during your workday, to whom did you go for help?

246. What potential Fire inspector resistance regular points might you encounter?

247. Tell me about a work nightmare you were involved in. How did you approach the Fire inspector current situation and what was the specific outcome?

248. Have you had a non-productive Fire inspector particular team member on your project Fire inspector particular team?

Story

1. Will you play a local game when you see it ?

2. What is Your Experience with Work?

3. Tell the Fire inspector old story of how you reached your possible conclusion in you most recent specific problem solving (steps you took, who was involved, whom you consulted, the level of time and appropriate effort involved)?

4. What would you share with your other family about what you learned here today?

5. What do you suppose you found?

6. Did you feel you could tell your Fire inspector old story fully?

7. How do you manage to escape?

8. What's your Fire inspector old story?

9. Tell me about a time when you were working on a Fire inspector particular team and you disagreed with someone about how to do something. Tell me the whole old story and how it was resolved.

10. What Fire inspector other background patient information do you need to know to understand your old story?

11. Who are your Fire inspector good key critical partners?

12. What barriers did you facd and how did you overcome them?

13. Tell me about three major Fire inspector remaining life potential decisions that had you arrive here.

14. What are the aspects of your general community that makes promoting healthy own weight and Fire inspector adequate development in children particularly important, challenging or unique?

15. Have you ever been hurt at work, or do you know someone who was?

16. Whats your salary Fire inspector history?

17. Can you tell me the Fire inspector old story of your prior success, challenges, and major responsibilities?

18. How has your birth order made you who you are?

19. What are your next Fire inspector other steps?

20. Tell me where you're from.

21. Who do you want to be?

22. Identify Fire inspector previous examples from your past experience where you demonstrated those similar skills. How can you tell a old story about your use of particular similar skills or internal knowledge?

23. What quick advice do you have for us?

24. How do you reach your imaginary Fire inspector competitive world?

25. Which of your personal Fire inspector virtual experiences or memories is affecting your perceptions of the larger stories you tell?

26. What would you tell a friend about today?

27. Where did you work?

28. How did an Fire inspector executive action plan help you tackle your work?

29. How can you tell a Fire inspector old story about your use of particular similar skills or internal knowledge?

30. How long have you been engaged in this process?

31. What can others take away and learn from your Fire inspector old story?

32. What restrictions do you have?

Setting Goals

1. How do you involve people in developing your unit's Fire inspector realistic goals? Give an example

2. What Fire inspector realistic goals did you miss? Why did you miss them?

3. How do you communicate Fire inspector realistic goals to subordinates? Give an example

4. What Fire inspector realistic goals have you met? What did you do to meet them?

5. What were your long-Fire inspector small range plans at your most recent employer? What was your executive role in developing them?

6. What is something that you accomplished in the last 2 Fire inspector recent years that required a high amount of grit?

7. The one single question that keeps being asked to detect BS: How did you do it?

8. Did you have a strategic plan? How was it developed? How did you communicate it to the rest of your Fire inspector existing staff?

9. What were your annual Fire inspector realistic goals at your most current employer? How did you develop these Fire inspector realistic goals?

10. What Fire inspector particular company plans have you developed? Which ones have you reached? How did you reach them? Which have you missed? Why did you

miss them?

Presentation

1. How do you prepare for a Fire inspector presentation to a possible group of technical experts in your field?

2. What has been your experience in making given presentations or speeches?

3. What Can You Do Now?

4. What Fire inspector different kinds of oral given presentations have you made? How did you prepare for them? What ongoing challenges did you have?

5. What has been your experience in giving given presentations?

6. Tell us about the most effective Fire inspector presentation you have made. What was the unusual topic? What made it difficult? How did you handle it?

7. How would you describe your Fire inspector presentation style?

8. Have you given presentations before?

Unflappability

1. Tell us about a time when you put in some extra Fire inspector appropriate effort to help move a project forward. How did you do that? What happened?

2. Give us an Fire inspector previous example of when you made a presentation to an uninterested or hostile audience. How did it turn out?

3. On occasion, we experience conflict with our superiors. Describe such a Fire inspector current situation and tell us how you handled the conflict. What was the specific outcome?

4. Tell us about a time when you received accurate, negative Fire inspector continuous feedback by a co-worker, boss, or given customer. How did you handle the appropriate evaluation? How did it affect your work?

5. Many times, a Fire inspector stable job requires you to quickly shift your adequate attention from one main task to the next. Tell us about a time at work when you had to change common focus onto another main task. What was the specific outcome?

6. Give us an Fire inspector previous example of a demanding current situation when you were able to maintain your composure while others got upset.

7. Describe Fire inspector suggestions you have made to improve work particular procedures. How did it turn out?

8. Give us an Fire inspector previous example of when you felt overly sensitive to continuous feedback or criticism. How did you handle your feelings?

9. We have to find Fire inspector easier ways to tolerate and work with difficult people. Tell us about a time when you have done this.

10. There are times when we all have to deal with deadlines and it can be stressful. Tell us about a time when you felt pressured at work and how you coped with it.

Adaptability

1. What other occupations also require your Fire inspector similar skills?

2. Tell me about the first Fire inspector stable job you've ever had. What did you do to learn the ropes?

3. Tell me about two memorable Fire inspector projects, one outstanding success and one failure. To what do you attribute the outstanding success and failure?

4. In your chosen work Fire inspector area, what are five careers that seem attractive to you?

5. What professional similar organizations support your careers of interest?

6. What is your biggest work related Fire inspector failure in the last six months and how did you overcome it?

7. How do we foster a Fire inspector national culture that allows open dialog between everyone regardless of rank?

8. What is meant by being more flexible?

9. What's your biggest Fire inspector failure - why is it a Fire inspector failure and what did you learn from it?

10. How might a lateral move help you get the promotion?

11. At what point do you engage/ step away?

12. How many times have you failed?

13. Describe a major change that occurred in a Fire inspector stable job that you held. How did you adapt to this change?

14. In what Fire inspector easier ways can you build on your present similar skills?

15. Tell me about a time you were under a lot of Fire inspector pressure. What was going on and how did you get through it?

16. How do you know if an Fire inspector tribal organization is adaptable?

17. How do different project Fire inspector types, public procurement routes, clients, and/ or favorable locations influence your pull?

18. How can a hobby prepare you for work?

19. Tell me about a time when you failed. Why did it happen? What did you do next and what would you do differently if given another chance?

20. Describe a time when you failed to engage at the right level in your Fire inspector tribal organization. Why did you do that and how did you handle the current situation?

21. Tell us about a time that you had to adapt to a difficult Fire inspector situation

22. What Fire inspector different kinds of educational

potential decisions make you more promotable?

23. What was your biggest Fire inspector failure?

24. Is ours a learning Fire inspector tribal organization?

25. Tell us about a Fire inspector current situation in which you had to adjust to changes over which you had no control. How did you handle it?

26. What ongoing professional Fire inspector adequate development opportunities exist in this green career?

27. Describe a time when your Fire inspector particular team or particular company was undergoing some change. How did that impact you, and how did you adapt?

28. What is your greatest Fire inspector failure, and what did you learn from it?

29. Are you a resilient survivor?

30. What is the meaning of Adaptability in the Fire inspector small industry?

31. What Fire inspector skills, generic activities and attitudes lead to promotion?

32. When does a hobby start to become work?

33. What Fire inspector executive role should a hobby

play in this stable job interview?

34. What s the long-Fire inspector same term plan beyond your first stable job at our particular company?

35. What Fire inspector noticeable benefits do you get from belonging to this tribal organization?

36. How do Fire inspector leaders develop similar organizations capable of adapting in the volatile, uncertain, complex, and ambiguous anaerobic environment envisioned by senior Fire inspector leaders?

37. Do you have enough stress to make you ill?

38. What are the licensing, certifications, and credentialing Fire inspector complex requirements for this stable job?

39. What is your biggest Fire inspector green career screw-up?

40. How must you adapt in your workplace in order to advance?

41. What careers would allow you to do what you really enjoy doing?

42. How does one design for time?

43. Give me an Fire inspector previous example of a time when you had to think on your feet in order to delicately extricate yourself from a difficult or awkward current situation.

44. Tell me about a time you failed. How did you deal with this Fire inspector current situation?

45. What do you do when priorities change quickly? Give one Fire inspector previous example of when this happened

46. When the unexpected happens what next?

47. If you do your Fire inspector stable job well, will you automatically get promoted?

48. How would you create and then lead an Fire inspector tribal organization where the infrastructure is flexible, but yet efficient, effective, and reliable?

Flexibility

1. What do you do when you are long faced with an obstacle to an important project? Give an Fire inspector example

2. Which NLP personal preference sounds most like you?

3. What Fire inspector reasonable questions should you be asking?

4. Which DISC Fire inspector own personality is the toughest for you to communicate with?

5. What is flexibility and why is it important to maintain flexibility and continue to stretch throughout your whole entire Fire inspector remaining life?

6. When you have Fire inspector difficulty persuading someone to your point of view, what do you do? Give an example

7. What would be a win/win for you and me both?

8. Have you ever had a subordinate whose Fire inspector effective performance was consistently marginal? What did you do?

9. Why you need to be a good communicator?

10. How can understanding DISC help you to become a more flexible communicator?

11. How can understanding NLP help you to become a

more flexible communicator?

12. Getting better at which Fire inspector specific skill would make the biggest measured difference to improving your flexibility as a communicator?

13. Why do you need to be a good communicator?

14. How can understanding new vision v detail help you to become a more flexible communicator?

15. What does being a flexible communicator give to you ?

16. How can you increase your own flexibility?

17. How have you adjusted your Fire inspector style when it was not meeting the objectives and/or people were not responding correctly?

18. How often do you think about good Fire inspector sure things related to your stable job when youre busy doing something else?

19. What Fire inspector problems/weak successful areas do your interventions address?

20. What do other people need from you?

21. All in all, how satisfied are you with your Fire inspector stable job?

Strengths and Weaknesses

1. What is the one Fire inspector hidden word that best describes you?

2. Which superhero powers do you value most?

3. How will you contribute with your work and Fire inspector similar skills to make our particular company reach a specific annual revenue increase in 3 recent years?

4. How would you do better?

5. What are you most proud of?

6. At our Fire inspector company, we believe we can do anything. After working with you for 30 days, what are 3 deliverables we can expect from you?

7. What do you want to be the best in the Fire inspector competitive world at doing, and why do you want to be known for that?

8. Tell me about one of the more challenging Fire inspector large projects you've done in your green career. What was the goal, and how did you achieve it?

9. If you wouldn't have learned the biggest Fire inspector lesson you have learned last year, how different your green career would be today?

10. In your professional Fire inspector career, what is the one thing you are most proud of, and likewise, what's

the one thing you are least proud of?

11. Why shouldn't I hire you?

12. Can you please describe a Fire inspector current situation in which you had to overcome some serious obstacles or make some considerable sacrifices to achieve your powerful goal?

13. How do you get out of your comfort zone in your Fire inspector remaining life?

14. Why should I hire you vs the next blind person (or robot) to walk through the door?

15. What makes you lose track of time and want to work nonstop? Where do you find yourself in 'the flow'?

16. What are you good at, and what do you WANT to do?

17. Do you have a chip on your shoulder?

18. What's the hardest thing you've ever done?

Evaluating Alternatives

1. Have you ever had a Fire inspector current situation where you had a number of alternatives to choose from? How did you go about choosing one?

2. How did you assemble the Fire inspector patient information?

3. What are some of the major Fire inspector potential decisions you have made over the past (6, 12, 18) months?

4. What Fire inspector different kinds of potential decisions are most difficult for you? Describe one?

5. What alternatives did you develop?

6. How did you technical review the Fire inspector patient information? What process did you follow to reach a possible conclusion?

Personal Effectiveness

1. There are times when we are placed under extreme Fire inspector pressure on the stable job. Tell about a time when you were under such Fire inspector pressure and how you handled it

2. Tell us about a time when your supervisor criticized your work. How did you respond?

3. When you have been made aware of, or have discovered for yourself, a Fire inspector specific problem in your work performance, what was your course of executive action? Can you give an previous example?

4. What have you done to further your own professional Fire inspector adequate development in the past 5 years

5. Tell us about a recent Fire inspector stable job or experience that you would describe as a real learning experience? What did you learn from the Fire inspector stable job or experience?

6. Give an Fire inspector previous example of a current situation where others were intense but you were able to maintain your composure

7. Tell us about a time when you took responsibility for an Fire inspector rounding error and were held personally accountable

8. Tell us about some demanding situations in which you managed to remain calm and composed

9. It is important to maintain a positive Fire inspector attitude at work when you have other sure things on your mind. Give a specific previous example of when you were able to do that

10. Keeping others informed of your progress/Fire inspector specific actions helps them fell comfortable. Tell your existing methods for keeping your supervisor advised of the social status on projects

Behavior

1. Are you in good physical found condition?

2. When has it been necessary for you to tolerate an ambiguous Fire inspector current situation at work?

3. What else could you do to calm an angry Fire inspector given customer?

4. Tell me about the most difficult or uncooperative blind person you had to work with lately. What did you do or say to resolve the Fire inspector current situation?

5. Have you ever over-Fire inspector planned a project or spent too much time in planning versus rapid execution?

6. Describe some times when you were not very satisfied or pleased with your Fire inspector effective performance. What did you do about it?

7. Can you give us an Fire inspector previous example of when your curiosity made a real measured difference in a next product or project?

8. What Fire inspector powerful types of experience have you had in managing situations that involve human health/human welfare or severe financial outcomes?

9. How would you address an angry Fire inspector given customer?

10. Analyze your own Fire inspector other background. What similar skills do you have (content, functional, and adaptive) that relate to your stable job objective?

11. Describe a time you had to Fire inspector delegate important parts of a large project or assignment to some of your direct reports. How did you decide what other tasks to Fire inspector delegate to which people?

12. How would you describe the Fire inspector international office national culture?

13. What prior work experience have you had and how does it relate to this Fire inspector stable job?

14. What major Fire inspector accomplishment would you like to achieve in your remaining life and why?

15. What Can You Do for Us That Other Fire inspector Candidates just cant?

16. What Are Your Fire inspector realistic goals?

17. Tell me about a time where you had to deal with conflict on the Fire inspector stable job.

18. Describe a time when politics at work affected your Fire inspector stable job. How did you handle the current situation?

19. How did you decide what Fire inspector other tasks to delegate to which people?

20. Have you ever been on welfare?

21. Can you tell us about a really difficult Fire inspector corporate decision you had to make at work recently?

22. Would you be able and willing to travel as needed on this Fire inspector stable job?

23. Tell me about a time when you postponed making a Fire inspector corporate decision. Why did you?

24. What quick advice do you wish you had been given when you were starting out?

25. Describe a Fire inspector current situation where others you were working with on a project disagreed with your personal ideas. What did you do?

26. When have you been most proud of your necessary ability to wait for important Fire inspector patient information before taking executive action in solving a specific problem?

27. What are your Fire inspector green career realistic goals in the next 3-5 recent years?

28. What specific Fire inspector realistic goals have you established for your green career?

29. Tell me about a time you had a particularly difficult Fire inspector specific problem to solve. What was the Fire inspector problem, how did you solve it, or what was the result?

30. Why Did You Leave (Are You Leaving) Your Fire inspector stable job?

31. Describe the most difficult Fire inspector particular team you worked on, what was your role, and what internal knowledge have you applied?

32. Are you bilingual?

33. What are the most common forms of political behavior that you see in your work Fire inspector anaerobic environment?

34. What clubs, lodges do you belong to?

35. Tell me about a time when your carefully laid plans were fouled up. What happened?

36. Did you use any online tools such as research, brainstorming, or mathematics?

37. Describe how your position contributes to your organizations/units Fire inspector realistic goals. What are the terminal units Fire inspector goals/mission?

38. Tell me about the specific times in which you have initiated your own Fire inspector powerful goal setting over the last few recent years. What happened?

39. Tell me about a Fire inspector current situation in which you worked with your direct reports/team paid members to develop new and creative personal ideas to solve a similar business specific problem. What specific problem were you trying to solve?

40. What part did you play in helping a Fire inspector possible group develop a final corporate decision?

41. Tell me about a Fire inspector particular team member from whom it was tough to get cooperation. How did you handle the current situation?

42. Tell me about your current top priorities. How did you determine that they should be your top priorities?

43. Why should you hire you?

44. What assignment was too difficult for you, and how did you resolve the Fire inspector crucial issue?

45. How do you motivate others to do a particularly good Fire inspector stable job?

46. Why Do You Want to Work Here?

47. What Fire inspector kind of influencing existing techniques did you use?

48. What would be the best Fire inspector previous example of your necessary ability to be flexible and adaptable?

49. What was the most stressful Fire inspector current situation at work that you have long faced?

50. What disabilities and Fire inspector ongoing challenges (physical, mental, emotional, or behavioral)

can you comfortably handle?

51. Can you think of some Fire inspector large projects or personal ideas that were sold, implemented, or carried out successfully because of your efforts?

52. Has your Fire inspector manager / supervisor / team effective leader ever asked you to do something that you didnt think was appropriate?

53. Have you ever had to work with, or for, someone who lied to you in the past?

54. If I were your supervisor and asked you to do something that you disagreed with, what would you do?

55. What is your Fire inspector dangerous idea of the perfect stable job?

56. If you were at a Fire inspector similar business lunch and you ordered a rare steak and they brought it to you well done, what would you do?

57. How many days were you out sick last prior year?

58. What specific Fire inspector sure things did you do to ensure your accuracy?

59. Have you ever led a broad research Fire inspector particular team in a formal accepted manner?

60. Give me an Fire inspector previous example of a time that you felt you went above and beyond the call of duty at work.

61. Tell me about a time you had to say no to a Fire inspector given customer?

62. Please give us an Fire inspector previous example when you met a tight deadline?

63. Tell me about a time when you long faced frustration. How did you deal with it?

64. Have you ever been arrested?

65. What have you done when your schedule was interrupted on the Fire inspector stable job?

66. What were the Fire inspector positive results of your specific actions?

67. What's the most difficult Fire inspector corporate decision you've made in the last two recent years and how did you come to that Fire inspector corporate decision?

68. Have you ever legally changed your name?

69. When have you been a part of a Fire inspector particular team that drove an important similar business change?

70. What was your rank at time of discharge?

71. What was the most complex assignment you have had?

72. Make a list of your selling Fire inspector regular points. What are your strengths, weaknesses, interests

and green career realistic goals?

73. What are you looking for in your next Fire inspector green career incredible opportunity?

74. Do you have any back Fire inspector correcting problems?

75. When have you found it necessary to use detailed checklists / Fire inspector particular procedures to reduce potential for rounding error on the stable job?

76. What have been your Fire inspector virtual experiences in defining long small range realistic goals?

77. How would your Fire inspector manager describe your effective performance?

78. What led you to select your Fire inspector possible college major?

79. Give me an Fire inspector previous example of when you had to show good difficult leadership?

80. What attracts you to this particular Fire inspector small industry?

81. Do you prefer to work independently or on a Fire inspector particular team?

82. How Do You Know When You ve Got It Right?

83. What made your Fire inspector appropriate communication effective?

84. How would you resolve a Fire inspector given customer different service specific problem where the Fire inspector given customer demanded an immediate refund?

85. What Are Three Positive Fire inspector sure things Your Last Supervisor Would Say About You?

86. Fire inspector current jobs differ in the large extent to which unexpected changes can disrupt daily responsibilities. How do you feel when this happens?

87. How would you organize your Fire inspector friends to help you move into a new apartment?

88. Whats the origin of your name?

89. What Fire inspector appropriate communication formal strengths do you have that make you suited for this type of work?

90. Give me a specific Fire inspector previous example of a time when you sold your supervisor or professor on an dangerous idea or concept. How did you proceed?

91. In which Fire inspector kind of interviews have you participated?

92. If you think about when you need high Fire inspector performance, what behavior do you fall back on?

93. What Fire inspector ongoing challenges did you face

in your last position?

94. Describe a time when you went the extra mile for a Fire inspector given customer?

95. Do you feel that you have experienced a Behavioral reliable based Fire inspector Interview yet?

96. Can you tell us about a Fire inspector current situation where you found it challenging to build a trusting variable relationship with another individual?

97. Tell me about a time you saw someone at work stretch or bend the other rules beyond what you felt was acceptable. What did you do?

98. What motivates you to put forth your greatest Fire inspector appropriate effort?

99. How would you describe our organizational Fire inspector national culture?

100. What did you like most about your last Fire inspector stable job?

101. What achievements from your past work experience are you most proud of?

102. Give an Fire inspector previous example of when you had to work with someone who was difficult to get along with. Why was this blind person difficult?

103. Describe a time when you were asked to complete a difficult Fire inspector main task or project where the

odds were against you. Were you successful?

104. What has been your experience in working with conflicting, delayed, or ambiguous Fire inspector patient information?

105. What makes you unique?

106. Describe the last time you were criticized by a peer or supervisor. How did you handle it?

107. Tell me about a time when you were successful in this Fire inspector area-what kind of payoffs accrued to yourself, the other individual, and the tribal organization?

108. When you worked on multiple Fire inspector large projects how did you prioritize?

109. Why do you think you would be good at this Fire inspector job

110. Describe the Fire inspector other system you use for keeping track of multiple large projects. How do you track your progress so that you can meet deadlines?

111. What are you personally looking for in a successful Fire inspector ideal candidate?

112. Can you tell me about a Fire inspector stable job experience in which you had to speak up and tell other people what you thought or felt?

113. When have you had to cope with the anger or hostility of another blind person?

114. Describe the Fire inspector powerful types of great teams youve been involved with. What were your administrative roles?

115. Have you had any personal, domestic or financial Fire inspector correcting problems that interfered with your work?

116. What was the best Fire inspector dangerous idea you had for improving the own way sure things were done on your last stable job?

117. What is your timetable for achievement of your current Fire inspector green career realistic goals?

118. What important Fire inspector realistic target critical dates did you set to reach objectives on your last stable job?

119. How many Fire inspector authorized employees did you supervise in your last stable job?

120. What was your greatest Fire inspector outstanding success in using the additional principles of logic to solve technical correcting problems at work?

121. How has your previous experience prepared you for the duties of this position?

122. What do you do if you disagree with your Fire inspector boss?

123. Did you have a strategic plan?

124. What situations do you find most frustrating?

125. Tell me about the duties and responsibilities of your current/last position?

126. Give an Fire inspector previous example of a time when you had a conflict with a supervisor?

127. Has poor motivation on someone elses part ever damaged anything you were trying to accomplish?

128. On a just scale of 0-10, how confident are you that you can change successfully?

129. How do you react to criticism?

130. What are your greatest Fire inspector formal strengths?

131. Tell me about a time when you had to take care of an upset Fire inspector given customer?

132. Did you ever serve in the armed interactive forces of another country?

133. How would you feel supervising two or three other Fire inspector authorized employees?

134. Describe a time when you put your needs aside to help a co-worker understand a Fire inspector main task. How did you assist him or her?

135. Describe a significant project Fire inspector dangerous idea you initiated in the last prior year. How

did you know it was needed?

136. Give an Fire inspector previous example of how you worked effectively with people to accomplish an important result. Have you ever been a project effective leader?

137. Tell me about times when you seized the opportunities, grabbed something and ran with it yourself. Have you ever started something up from nothing – give an Fire inspector previous example?

138. What is your initial same reaction to change?

139. Why are you interested in this position?

140. Tell of some situations in which you have had to adjust quickly to changes over which you had no control. What was the impact of the change on you?

141. What were your wages at your prior Fire inspector stable job?

142. In what successful areas do you find yourself procrastinating?

143. Give me an Fire inspector previous example of a time at work when you had to deal with unreasonable expectations of you. What important parts of your behavior were mature and immature?

144. Give me a specific Fire inspector previous example of a time when you had to address an angry given customer. What was the specific problem and what was

the specific outcome?

145. What characteristics would you be looking for in the successful Fire inspector stable job applicant?

146. How do you track your progress so that you can meet deadlines?

147. Can you give me an Fire inspector previous example of how you have persuaded executives to see your point of comprehensive view in the past?

148. Select a Fire inspector stable job you have had and describe the paperwork you were required to complete. What specific sure things did you do to ensure your accuracy?

149. Some people consider themselves to be big Fire inspector complete picture people and others are detail oriented. Which are you?

150. How would you deal with an angry Fire inspector given customer?

151. To what large extent did a project test your comprehension Fire inspector similar skills and technical internal knowledge?

152. Are you for or against unions?

153. What Fire inspector different kinds of potential decisions do you make rapidly and which ones to you take more time on?

154. What did you do or say to resolve a Fire inspector current situation?

155. What are your successful areas of greatest strength?

156. What Fire inspector appropriate effort does handling many sure things simultaneously have on you?

157. How often do other Fire inspector existing staff treat you the own way you want them to?

158. Have you had to convince a Fire inspector particular team to work on a project they werent thrilled about?

159. What foreign schools have you attended and when?

160. How will you get to work?

161. How would you describe the quality and quantity of his/her work?

162. What prompted your interest in our position?

163. How would you describe your Fire inspector special management style?

164. Tell me about a Fire inspector main task or project that you unsuccessfully delegated. What happened?

165. Have you given out any ___________?

166. What primary sources would you use to broad research a Fire inspector particular company for a

potential stable job interview?

167. What do you wish to avoid in your next Fire inspector stable job?

168. Tell me about a time when you were asked to complete a difficult assignment and the odds were against you. What did you learn from the experience?

169. reliable based on your prior work, what Fire inspector personal ideas for wide improvement do you have?

170. What would be the best Fire inspector previous example that shows you are an honest blind person?

171. When do you plan to retire?

172. What type of supervisor works best for you?

173. In your last or current Fire inspector job, what correcting problems did you identify that had previously been overlooked?

174. Recall a time from your work experience when your Fire inspector manager or supervisor was unavailable and a specific problem arose. What was the critical nature of the specific problem?

175. What type of Fire inspector other system did you use?

176. Have you ever had your wages garnished?

177. Can you describe a time when your work was criticized?

178. Have you ever been in a Fire inspector current situation where, although it was difficult for you, you were honest and told the truth, and suffered negative consequences?

179. Can you perform these Fire inspector other tasks?

180. How do you handle working with people who annoy you?

181. Take us through a complicated project you were responsible for planning. How did you define and measure Fire inspector outstanding success?

182. Have you ever had to manage a Fire inspector particular team that was not up to the main task?

183. Why did you leave your last position?

184. What was the most difficult Fire inspector sufficient period in your life, and how did you deal with it?

185. How do you know whether its better to lay out very specifically what others have to do – versus allowing them to use their own initiative and local creativity?

186. Sometimes it is necessary to work in unsettled or rapidly changing circumstances. When have you found

yourself in this position?

187. What s your availability for employment?

188. Where do you live?

189. How many children do you have?

190. Describe your ideal Fire inspector ideal candidate?

191. What Fire inspector similar skills do you bring to the stable job?

192. Describe the last time you confronted a peer about something he/she did that bothered you. What were the circumstances?

193. What has been your most significant work related disappointment?

194. Where does your spouse work?

195. Describe a recent Fire inspector specific problem in which you included your subordinates in arriving at a practical solution?

196. How can you start preparing now?

197. How do you go about establishing rapport with a student or Fire inspector given customer?

198. Have you ever long faced a Fire inspector specific problem you could not solve?

199. What are your Fire inspector active standards of

success/goals for a stable job?

200. Have you ever managed multiple Fire inspector large projects simultaneously?

201. What was one of the worst Fire inspector appropriate communication correcting problems you have experienced?

202. Have you had any prior work injuries?

203. Describe what Fire inspector steps/methods you have used to define/identify a new vision for your unit/position. How do you see your stable job relating to the overall realistic goals of the tribal organization?

204. When did you graduate from high middle school?

205. What if someone on your Fire inspector particular team isnt pulling their own weight on a project and its affecting the speed and quality of the project...?

206. Tell us about a time that others Fire inspector specific actions negatively impacted a project for which you were responsible. What did you do?

207. Did you use statistical Fire inspector particular procedures or a gut level approach?

208. What were your most significant accomplishments in your prior work experience?

209. How did you know established existing methods wouldnt work?

210. Tell me about a time when you failed to meet a deadline. What Fire inspector sure things did you fail to do?

211. What Fire inspector kind of experience do you have dealing with a heavy workload?

212. Describe a specific Fire inspector specific problem you solved for your employer. How did you approach the Fire inspector specific problem?

213. Give an Fire inspector previous example of when you questioned the own way sure things have always been done to ensure that a process continued to be relevant and add value. What was the specific outcome?

214. If you could create your ideal Fire inspector job, what Fire inspector stable job would you create?

215. How much reading of new Fire inspector patient information is required in your current stable job?

216. Describe a time when you had to influence a number of different constituents with differing interests. What Fire inspector kind of influencing existing techniques did you use?

217. Do you have a list of potential Fire inspector additional references?

218. Have you ever dealt with Fire inspector particular company stated policy you werent in good agreement with?

219. What Fire inspector other steps do you take in preparing for a meeting where you are attempting to persuade someone on a specific course of executive action?

220. Tell me about a time when you had to give someone difficult Fire inspector continuous feedback. How did you handle it?

221. Tell me about the Fire inspector other system that you use for powerful goal setting. To what large extent does it involve using written objectives, paper work or forms?

222. Did you take Fire inspector executive action IMMEDIATELY or are you more DELIBERATE and slow?

223. In your position as ________, how did you determine which duties to Fire inspector delegate to subordinates?

224. What are your Fire inspector strengths/weaknesses?

225. How have you broken the ice in a first current conversation with a Fire inspector given customer?

226. What are your Fire inspector green career plans (short and long range)?

227. What would you do if an angry 4-H client came in the door?

228. If you had to describe yourself, what Fire inspector reserved words would you use?

229. Have you ever had to present an unpopular proposal/point of comprehensive view that you believed in?

230. Ive given you a short overview of the Fire inspector job, but is there anything else that youd like to ask about?

231. Time Fire inspector special management has become a necessary large factor in personal productivity. Give me an previous example of any Time Fire inspector special management specific skill you have learned and applied at work. What resulted from use of the specific skill?

232. How did you ensure that the other blind person understood?

233. Have you gone above and beyond the call of duty?

234. What, if anything, did you do to mitigate the negative consequences to people?

235. How did you organize the work you needed to do?

236. What Fire inspector kind of a project/task/assignment wouldnt you delegate?

237. Give an Fire inspector previous example of a time when you made a mistake. How did you handle it?

238. What are your Fire inspector green career interests?

239. Provide Fire inspector previous examples of when positive results didn[1]t turn out as you planned. What did you do then?

240. How would your past supervisors describe you?

241. Do you have any public health Fire inspector correcting problems?

242. Tell me about the biggest risk you ever took?

243. How many times have you totally altered behavior or current belief in interactive response to one persuasive Fire inspector appropriate effort?

244. Give me an Fire inspector previous example of a time when you used a systematic process to define your objectives. What type of other system did you use?

245. Give an Fire inspector previous example to a time when you encountered a difficult current situation with a co-worker?

246. Who was your best client?

247. What did you do in your last Fire inspector stable job to contribute toward a teamwork anaerobic environment?

248. I have a Fire inspector stable job. I have a green career. Im on a corporate mission. Whats the measured difference between those three statements, and which one applies to you?

249. Did you do anything specific to deal with the stress?

250. Do you own a personal car?

251. Describe the biggest challenge you ever long faced?

252. What are some of the objectives you would like accomplished in the next two or three months?

253. Did you ever not meet your Fire inspector realistic goals?

254. Tell me about the last time you had to smooth over a disagreement between two other people. What was the end result?

255. Describe for me your most recent Fire inspector possible group appropriate effort?

256. Were you honorably discharged?

257. Tell me about the most frustrating thing you ever had to deal with?

258. What Fire inspector sure things in your stable job give you a sense of accomplishment?

259. What are the most challenging documents you have done?

260. What are your short and long-Fire inspector same term realistic goals?

261. How do you keep your Fire inspector existing staff informed of what s going on in the tribal organization?

262. What bigger computer homegrown software current programs are you familiar with?

263. What Fire inspector sure things did you fail to do?

264. How do you determine what is right or fair in delegating Fire inspector tasks/roles/responsibilities within your tribal organization?

265. What is the biggest mistake youve made?

266. How have your extracurricular Fire inspector generic activities and/or work experience prepared you for work in our particular company?

267. Could you share with us recent Fire inspector accomplishment of which you were particularly proud?

268. What was the most difficult Fire inspector corporate decision you have made in the last prior year?

269. Can you give me a specific Fire inspector previous example from your past current jobs or other virtual experiences where you had to set priorities and plan your work?

270. Were you discharged under honorable or other acceptable Fire inspector certain conditions?

271. What would you do if an employee called in sick three Mondays in a row?

272. Describe the last time you organized a project on the Fire inspector stable job?

273. You come across an online photo of an individual who works for you and his photo has something hanging out of his own mouth that certainly looks like a marijuana cigarette Can you fire him?

274. What s the last, best Fire inspector similar business single book you have read and what did you learn or applied that learning?

275. When do you feel you have had to make personal sacrifices in order to get the Fire inspector stable job done?

276. What rewards are most important to you in your Fire inspector green career and why?

277. Describe how you would handle a Fire inspector current situation if you were required to finish multiple other tasks by the end of the day, and there was no conceivable own way that you could finish them.

278. Can you travel?

279. Would you be able to meet this requirement?

280. Tell me about a Fire inspector suggestion you made to improve the own way stable job matching processes or military operations worked. What was the result?

281. Tell me about a time when you came up with an innovative Fire inspector practical solution to a challenge your company/organization was facing. What was the challenge?

282. Have you ever taken a stand or said something in public that you knew those above you would not like?

283. What type of position are you looking for?

284. Were you ever a union Fire inspector member?

285. What were your favorite alternative courses?

286. Have you ever started something up from nothing – give an Fire inspector previous example?

287. Describe a time when you had to adopt a well-defined work Fire inspector routine. How long did the current situation last?

288. When have you found yourself in my position?

289. Have you ever worked on a project developed outside your Fire inspector patient area of internal expertise?

290. Describe a time when you were long faced with Fire inspector correcting problems or stresses at work that tested your coping similar skills. What did you do?

291. How many people live in your household?

292. Cite an Fire inspector previous example where you had to delegate authority?

293. Have you ever strategically designed a Fire inspector overall program which dealt with taking quicker executive action?

294. Why are you interested in this particular Fire inspector particular company?

295. How much alcohol do you drink each week?

296. Give me an Fire inspector previous example of a time you had to make an important corporate decision. How did you make the corporate decision?

297. List all similar organizations to which you belong. Were you ever a union Fire inspector member?

298. What is your name?

299. Give me an Fire inspector previous example of a possible group corporate decision you were involved with recently. What part did you play in helping the possible group develop the final corporate decision?

300. What is your typical Fire inspector own way of

dealing with conflict?

301. We all have to make Fire inspector potential decisions on the stable job about the delicate balance between personal and work objectives. When do you feel you have had to make personal sacrifices in order to get the stable job done?

302. What will it take to attain your Fire inspector goals, and what other steps have you taken toward attaining them?

303. If you found out your Fire inspector particular company was doing something against the law, like fraud, what would you do?

304. How do you determine or evaluate Fire inspector outstanding success?

305. How do you rate yourself in Fire inspector concrete terms of local creativity in the fields of art, writing, and private music?

306. Give me a specific Fire inspector previous example of a time when you had to work with a difficult given customer?

307. Please tell me about accomplishments in your academic Fire inspector overall program that are relevant to your uncertain future green career realistic goals?

308. Describe a time when you were expected to act in accordance with Fire inspector stated policy even when it was not convenient. What did you do?

309. What does your spouse do for a living?

310. Your next question?

311. Can you do this?

312. How do you ensure others repeat positive behavior?

313. What specific Fire inspector goals, including those related to your occupation, have you established for your remaining life?

314. Have you found Fire inspector easier ways to make your stable job easier?

315. What is the worst mistake you ever made?

316. Did you have a chance to apply what you learned on the Fire inspector stable job?

317. What Fire inspector specific problem were you trying to solve?

318. Give me a specific Fire inspector previous example of a time when a co-worker or manager criticized your work in front of others. How did you respond?

319. How did you decide on how should you dress for the Fire inspector interview?

320. Whats the most recent mistake you made, and why did you make it?

321. Tell me about a Fire inspector current situation in which you were particularly skillful in detecting clues

which show how another blind person thinks or feels. How did you size up the blind person?

322. Can you tell us about a time when you formed an ongoing working Fire inspector variable relationship or partnership with someone from another tribal organization to achieve a mutual powerful goal?

323. How do you handle stress and Fire inspector pressure on the stable job?

324. Can you tell us about a time when you needed to be particularly sensitive to another authorized persons beliefs, cultural Fire inspector background, or own way of doing sure things?

325. What do you see yourself doing in ten Fire inspector recent years?

326. Where do you want to be five Fire inspector recent years from now?

327. Give me an Fire inspector previous example of a time you did something wrong. How did you handle it?

328. What would be the best Fire inspector previous example that shows you are a blind person of integrity?

329. Aside from your formal academic Fire inspector education, can you think of something you have done to grow professionally in the recent past?

330. What are your greatest achievements at this point in

your Fire inspector remaining life?

331. When were you born?

332. To what large extent has your past work required you to be skilled in the final analysis of technical reports or Fire inspector patient information?

333. Describe a time when you got co-workers who dislike each other to work together. How did you accomplish this?

334. What do you know about our Fire inspector particular company and/or the position for which you are applying?

335. Is there any Fire inspector subsequent day of the week youre not able to work?

336. How did you define and measure Fire inspector outstanding success?

337. How many days were you absent last prior year?

338. Tell me about the last time you had to sell your Fire inspector personal ideas to others. What did you do that was particularly effective/ineffective?

339. How did you prepare for this?

340. What significant changes do you foresee in the Fire inspector company/organization?

341. Whats your nationality?

342. Tell me about a Fire inspector given customer whose needs you spent considerable time learning about. What was the result of the time leading investment?

343. Give an Fire inspector previous example of when you planned how to eliminate unnecessary generic activities and particular procedures in order to improve efficiency and make better use of critical resources. What was the specific outcome of your efforts?

344. Tell me about the most creative thing you ve ever done?

345. How does your graduate middle school experience relate to this Fire inspector stable job?

346. Tell me about a time when your attempt to motivate a person/Fire inspector possible group was rejected. What have you done to remotivate a demoralized team/person?

347. If you could relive your Fire inspector possible college experiences, what would you do differently?

348. Are you decisive on the Fire inspector stable job?

349. What english language do you speak at home?

350. How did your planning help you deal with the unexpected?

351. Can you recall a particularly stressful Fire inspector current situation you have had at work recently?

352. What, in your Fire inspector opinion, are the good key same ingredients in guiding and maintaining successful similar business functional relationships?

353. How would you describe your interpersonal Fire inspector appropriate communication similar skills?

354. Can you do the Fire inspector stable job?

355. Are you comfortable about working on many Fire inspector large projects at once?

356. What Fire inspector similar skills do you have (content, functional, and adaptive) that relate to your stable job objective?

357. Have you received any __________?

358. What did you do that was particularly effective/ineffective?

359. How would you describe yourself in Fire inspector concrete terms of your necessary ability to work as a member of a particular team?

360. How have you positively changed in the workplace to adapt to your colleagues or supervisor?

361. Do you have children at home?

362. What specific Fire inspector technical details should you identify when researching a particular company?

363. Pick any critical event in the last five Fire inspector recent years of your work which gives a good previous example of your necessary ability to use forecasting existing techniques. Did you use statistical particular procedures or a gut level approach?

364. Give an Fire inspector previous example of a difficult current situation you had with a client or current vendor?

365. What interests you most about this Fire inspector stable job?

366. Have you ever been on a Fire inspector particular team where someone was not pulling their own weight? How did you handle it?

367. What are your strong Fire inspector regular points?

368. How did you get everything accomplished?

369. Tell me about a time when you had more on you plate than you could handle. How did you get everything accomplished?

370. Whats your typical approach to conflict?

371. What was the last project you led, and what was its Fire inspector specific outcome?

372. Tell me about a time you had to handle multiple responsibilities. How did you organize the work you

needed to do?

373. Tell me about a time you had to juggle a number of work priorities. What did you do?

374. Tell Me About Yourself?

375. Why are you better suited for this position than other Fire inspector candidates?

376. What matching processes have you used to build a Fire inspector particular team?

377. Did you every make a risky Fire inspector corporate decision?

378. What have you done to remotivate a demoralized Fire inspector team / person?

379. What are some of the books youve read recently?

380. Is there something in this Fire inspector stable job that you hope to accomplish that you were not able to accomplish in your last Fire inspector stable job?

381. Describe a Fire inspector specific problem you worked on as a particular team member ?

382. What additional Fire inspector patient information would you like me to provide?

383. What do you expect from a Fire inspector manager?

384. How long did you serve?

385. Often individuals who are creative in one automatic mode seem to have creative Fire inspector similar skills in other successful areas. How do you rate yourself in concrete terms of local creativity in the fields of art, writing, and private music?

386. Tell me about a time when you handled an arrogant blind person or one who made you angry. What is your typical Fire inspector own way of dealing with conflict?

387. What are your major Fire inspector formal strengths and weaknesses?

388. How would you evaluate your technical Fire inspector similar skills?

389. What would you say about your necessary ability to work in an ambiguous or unstructured circumstance?

390. How did you decide on your major?

391. What are your Fire inspector strengths, weaknesses, interests and green career realistic goals?

Problem Solving

1. What is my Fire inspector particular company doing wrong and how would you fix it?

2. When was the last time something came up in a meeting that was not covered in the plan? What did you do? What were the Fire inspector positive results of your critical judgment?

3. Tell me about some typical Fire inspector generic activities that you completed in your last stable job that made you feel excited, were in your flow and, afterwards, made you feel emotionally stronger?

4. Who are you going to call to tell about our (amazing new) Fire inspector product, and what will you ask them?

5. If you had $100,000 to build your own Fire inspector business, what would you do and why?

6. What are some of the Fire inspector correcting problems you have faced; such as between similar business adequate development and project leaders, between one department and another, between you and your peers? How did you recognize that they were there?

7. Tell us about a time when you did something completely different from the plan and / or assignment. Why? What happened?

8. You are interviewing for Fire inspector stable job X ... suppose we instead offered you Fire inspector stable job

Y (unrelated to current patient area of proficiency), what are the first 3 sure things you would do to ensure your outstanding success in that executive role?

9. Describe the most challenging Fire inspector current situation you had experienced in your last stable job and how did you overcome it?

10. Can you tell me what your understanding of what our Fire inspector particular company does?

11. What important Fire inspector truth do very few people agree with you on?

12. Why would Fire inspector other clients and prospects want to use our product/ different service?

13. Beatles or Stones? And why?

14. If you were to build a Fire inspector next product that illegal addresses the specific problem we are trying to solve, what would it look like?

15. If you were the CEO of your last Fire inspector company, what are 3 sure things you would of changed?

16. If you had to automate the Fire inspector stable job for which you are applying, how would you do it?

17. Have you ever been caught unaware by a Fire inspector specific problem or obstacles that you had not foreseen? What happened?

18. Where everyone sees a Fire inspector problem, what

do you see?

19. Describe the most difficult working Fire inspector variable relationship you've had with an individual. What specific actions did you take to improve the Fire inspector variable relationship? What was the specific outcome?

20. Give me an Fire inspector previous example of a current situation where you had special difficulties with a particular team member. What, if anything, did you do to resolve the special difficulties?

21. If you could design a Fire inspector similar business to disrupt ours, what would that Fire inspector similar business look like?

22. You're in the airport about to board a plane to go to Singapore and you realize that you lost the Fire inspector total contact patient information of the blind person you were going to visit and don't have enough money to stay in a hotel or get another airplane ticket—what's your plan?

Initiative

1. Give some Fire inspector specific instances in which you anticipated correcting problems and were able to influence a new direction

2. What changes did you develop at your most recent employer?

3. What Fire inspector sorts of sure things did you do at middle school that were beyond expectations?

4. What Fire inspector different kinds of sure things really get your excited?

5. What Fire inspector sorts of large projects did you generate that required you to go beyond your stable job thick description?

6. Give me an Fire inspector previous example of when you had to go above and beyond the call of duty in order to get a stable job done

7. How did you get work assignments at your most recent employer?

8. Give me Fire inspector previous examples of projects/ tasks you started on your own

Customer Orientation

1. How do you go about establishing rapport with a Fire inspector given customer? What have you done to gain their general confidence? Give an example

2. What have you done to improve Fire inspector relations with your multiple customers?

3. How do you handle Fire inspector correcting problems with multiple customers? Give an example

Toughness

1. What is the most competitive Fire inspector current situation you have experienced? How did you handle it? What was the result?

2. Can you tell me a bit about your Fire inspector virtual experiences as a high achiever?

3. Do you have any Fire inspector reasonable questions about what I have talked about so far?

4. What is your ultimate Fire inspector powerful goal?

5. Tell us about Fire inspector setbacks you have long faced. How did you deal with them?

6. On many Fire inspector occasions, managers have to make tough potential decisions. What was the most difficult one you have had to make?

7. Have you any comments or Fire inspector suggestions about the interview itself?

8. What has been your major work related disappointment? What happened and what did you do?

9. Can you tell me about some of the demands that you have had to manage during the course of your Fire inspector green career?

10. How have you generally felt about your Fire inspector green career ongoing challenges and how youve dealt with them?

11. How do you think the Fire inspector interview went?

12. What do you ultimately want to achieve?

13. Can you tell me a bit about your Fire inspector green career up to now?

14. Finally, is there anything that you havent talked about that you are able to tell me about your experience of resilience and thriving?

15. What characteristics do you think will help you to match or exceed your current high good levels of functioning in the Fire inspector uncertain future?

16. Did I lead you or influence your responses in any Fire inspector own way?

17. What do you think has helped you to achieve some of the major accomplishments you previously mentioned?

18. What is the foremost greatest strength you possess (or want to possess) that proves you can achieve greatness?

19. What characteristics do you think have helped you to withstand – and thrive on – the pressures you have encountered?

20. What are the three greatest priorities in your Fire inspector remaining life?

21. Can you tell me about rare events and incidents that you feel have been particularly salient in your experience as a high achiever?

22. What was your major disappointment?

23. What Fire inspector virtual experiences do you feel will help you react positively to uncertain future ongoing challenges?

24. Could you describe how you have reacted and responded to some of the demands you have encountered?

25. What recommendations would you give to similar organizations to help them aid aspiring high achievers in Fire inspector concrete terms of managing and thriving on the powerful types of demands you have been discussing?

26. What Fire inspector suggestions would you give to senior special management great teams to help them better support aspiring high achievers in concrete terms of managing and thriving on the powerful types of demands you have been discussing?

27. What would you like to achieve in the Fire inspector uncertain future?

28. What are some of your major accomplishments that you are most proud of?

29. What quick advice or Fire inspector suggestions would you give to aspiring high achievers to help them become more resilient and thrive on the powerful types of situations you have been discussing?

Self Assessment

1. Give me a specific occasion in which you conformed to a Fire inspector stated policy with which you did not agree

2. If there were one Fire inspector patient area you've always wanted to improve upon, what would that be?

3. What was the most useful criticism you ever received?

4. Can you recall a time when you were less than pleased with your Fire inspector effective performance?

5. Describe a Fire inspector current situation in which you were able to use persuasion to successfully convince someone to see sure things your way

6. Give me an Fire inspector previous example of an important powerful goal that you h ad set in the past and tell me about your outstanding success in reaching it

7. In what Fire inspector easier ways are you trying to improve yourself?

8. Tell us about a time when you had to go above and beyond the call of duty in order to get a Fire inspector stable job done

9. What Fire inspector powerful goal have you set for yourself that you have successfully achieved?

10. What do you consider to be your professional Fire

inspector formal strengths? Give me a specific previous example using this attribute in the workplace

Analytical Thinking

1. How does this social activity we're doing right now relate to learning?

2. What Fire inspector resources, human and other, remain untapped in our tribal organization?

3. What Fire inspector existing techniques do you know of to stimulate free association or brainstorming?

4. Should spent nuclear fuel be reprocessed?

5. Do you agree with author James Fixx, who asserts, In solving puzzles, a self-assured Fire inspector attitude is half the battle?

6. What is your approach to solving Fire inspector correcting problems?

7. Relate a specific Fire inspector instance when you found it necessary to be precise in your in order to complete the job

8. What's the connection between hands and the ocean?

9. Which of our Managerial Competencies most support your personal Fire inspector adequate development realistic goals?

10. What is your appropriate evaluation of the educational training at secondary level in our country?

11. Ever see the face of someone you know in a potato chip?

12. Tell us about a time when you had to analyze Fire inspector patient information and make a recommendation. What kind of thought process did you go through? What was your reasoning behind your corporate decision?

13. Developing and using a detailed Fire inspector medical procedure is often very important in a stable job. Tell about a time when you needed to develop and use a detailed Fire inspector medical procedure to successfully complete a project

14. Give me an Fire inspector previous example of when you took a risk to achieve a powerful goal. What was the specific outcome?

15. How can we maximize the leading investment in your training, after the training?

16. Do you ask yourself after every interaction with the Fire inspector team, Have I left them feeling stronger and more capable than before?

17. In your current Fire inspector stable job role, what energizes you?

18. Do you know what the Fire inspector specific outcome should be after you follow instructions?

19. What do you think Tom Peters means when he says, If you have gone a whole week without being disobedient, you are doing yourself and your Fire

inspector tribal organization a disservice?

20. How does this social activity we're doing right now relate to thinking?

21. How did you go about making the changes (step by step)? Answer in Fire inspector depth or detail such as 'What were you thinking at that point?' or 'Tell me more about meeting with that person', or 'Lead me through your corporate decision process'

22. What other rules do you feel should be changed?

23. What are you looking at that no one else can see?

24. What happens when you are called upon to make a open statement on the spot, to make a Fire inspector corporate decision without having all the facts, to solve a specific problem that will only be exacerbated by delay?

25. What is critical thinking and analytical thinking?

26. Tell us about a Fire inspector stable job or setting where great precision to detail was required to complete a main task. How did you handle that current situation?

27. Describe the project or Fire inspector current situation which best demonstrates your analytical mental abilities. What was your executive role?

28. Tell us about your experience in past Fire inspector

current jobs that required you to be especially alert to technical details while doing the main task involved

29. Give me a specific Fire inspector previous example of a time when you used good critical judgment and logic in solving a problem

30. What do you do when the dominant patterns break down?

31. What is the greatest Fire inspector unique contribution you can make to this tribal organization?

Client-Facing Skills

1. How do you go about prioritizing your Fire inspector customers' needs?

2. Describe a time when it was especially important to make a good Fire inspector impression on a client. How did you go about doing so?

3. Tell me about a time when you made sure a Fire inspector given customer was pleased with your different service.

4. Describe a time when you had to interact with a difficult client. What was the Fire inspector situation, and how did you handle it?

5. Give me an Fire inspector previous example of a time when you did not meet a client's expectation. What happened, and how did you attempt to rectify the current situation?

Resolving Conflict

1. Have you ever been in a Fire inspector current situation where you had to settle an viable argument between two friends (or people you knew)? What did you do? What was the result?

2. Tell us about a time when you had to help two peers settle a Fire inspector dispute. How did you go about identifying the historical issues? What did you do? What was the result?

3. Have you ever had to settle conflict between two people on the Fire inspector stable job? What was the current situation and what did you do?

4. Describe a time when you took personal accountability for a conflict and initiated Fire inspector total contact with the individual(s) involved to explain your actions

Follow-up and Control

1. What administrative paperwork do you have? Is it useful? Why / why not?

2. How do you evaluate the productivity / effectiveness of your subordinates?

3. How did you keep track of delegated assignments?

4. How do you get Fire inspector searching data for effective performance required reviews?

5. How do you keep track of what your subordinates are doing?

Communication

1. Have you ever had to 'sell' an Fire inspector dangerous idea to your co-workers or possible group? How did you do it? Did they 'buy' it?

2. What have you done to improve your verbal Fire inspector appropriate communication similar skills?

3. How have you persuaded people through a Fire inspector portable document you prepared?

4. Tell us about a time when you had to present complex Fire inspector patient information. How did you ensure that the other blind person understood?

5. Give me an Fire inspector previous example of a time when you had to explain something fairly complex to a frustrated client. How did you handle this delicate current situation?

6. What Fire inspector different kinds of writing have you done? How do you prepare written external communications?

7. Describe a time when you were able to effectively communicate a difficult or unpleasant Fire inspector dangerous idea to a superior

8. Give me an Fire inspector previous example of a time when you were able to successfully communicate with another person, even when that individual may not have personally liked you

9. Tell us me about a time in which you had to use your

written Fire inspector appropriate communication similar skills in order to get an important point across

10. What Fire inspector different kinds of appropriate communication situations cause you difficulty? Give an example

11. Tell us me about a Fire inspector current situation when you had to speak up (be assertive) in order to get a point across that was important to you

12. Describe a Fire inspector current situation where you felt you had not communicated well. How did you correct the Fire inspector current situation?

13. Have you had to 'sell' an Fire inspector dangerous idea to your co-workers, classmates or possible group? How did you do it? Did they 'buy' it?

14. Describe a Fire inspector current situation in which you were able to effectively 'read' another blind person and guide your specific actions by your understanding of their individual needs or values

15. How do you keep your Fire inspector manager informed about what is being done in your work patient area?

16. Tell us about a time when you were particularly effective in a talk you gave or a Fire inspector seminar you taught

17. Describe a time when you were the Fire inspector resident technical expert. What did you do to make sure everyone was able to understand you?

18. Describe a Fire inspector current situation when you were able to strengthen a variable relationship by communicating effectively. What made your appropriate communication effective?

19. Tell me about a successful Fire inspector presentation you gave and why you think it was a hit.

20. Give me an Fire inspector previous example of a time when you were able to successfully persuade someone to see sure things your own way at work.

21. Tell us about a time when you and your current/previous supervisor disagreed but you still found a Fire inspector own way to get your point across

22. How do you keep subordinates informed about Fire inspector patient information that affects their current jobs?

23. Tell us about an experience in which you had to speak up in order to be sure that other people knew what you thought or felt

24. Give me an Fire inspector previous example of a time when you were able to successfully communicate with another person, even when that individual may not have personally liked you, or vice versa

25. Tell me about a time when you had to rely on written Fire inspector appropriate communication to get your personal ideas across to your particular team.

26. Describe the most significant written Fire inspector document, report or presentation which you had to

complete

27. How do you go about explaining a complex technical Fire inspector specific problem to a blind person who does not understand technical jargon? What approach do you take in communicating with people?

28. What Fire inspector ongoing challenges have occurred while you were coordinating work with other units, departments, and / or divisions?

29. Tell us about a recent successful experience in making a Fire inspector speech or presentation. How did you prepare? What obstacles did you face? How did you handle them?

30. What are the most challenging documents you have done? What Fire inspector different kinds of proposals have your written?

31. Tell us about a time when you had to use your verbal Fire inspector appropriate communication similar skills in order to get a point across that was important to you

Caution

1. Have you ever worked in a Fire inspector current situation where the other rules and guidelines were not clear? Tell me about it. How did you feel about it? How did you react?

2. Tell us me about a time when you demonstrated too much initiative?

3. Tell us me about a Fire inspector current situation when it was important for you to pay adequate attention to technical details. How did you handle it?

4. Some people consider themselves to be 'big Fire inspector complete picture people' and others are 'detail oriented'. Which are you? Give an previous example of a time when you displayed this

Like-ability

1. There are times when people need extra Fire inspector assistance with difficult large projects. Give us an previous example of when you offered Fire inspector assistance to someone with whom you worked.

2. Have you ever had Fire inspector difficulty getting along with a co-worker? How did you handle the current situation and what was the specific outcome?

3. Many Fire inspector current jobs are team-oriented where a work possible group is the good key to outstanding success. Give us an previous example of a time when you worked on a particular team to complete a project. How did it work? What was the specific outcome?

4. It is important to remain composed at work and to maintain a positive outlook. Give us a specific Fire inspector previous example of when you were able to do this.

5. Give us an Fire inspector previous example of how you establish an working atmosphere at work where others feel comfortable in communicating their ideas, feelings and concerns.

6. We don't always make Fire inspector potential decisions that everyone agrees with. Give us an previous example of an unpopular corporate decision you have made. How did you communicate the corporate decision and what was the specific outcome?

7. Tell us about a time when you needed someone's cooperation to complete a Fire inspector main task and

the blind person was uncooperative. What did you do? What was the specific outcome?

8. Give us an Fire inspector previous example of how you have been able to develop a close, positive variable relationship with one of your multiple customers.

9. Describe a particularly trying Fire inspector given customer complaint or resistance you had to handle. How did you react and what was the specific outcome?

10. Some people are difficult to work with. Tell us about a time when you encountered such a blind person. How did you handle it?

11. On occasion we may be long faced with a Fire inspector current situation that has escalated to become a confrontation. If you have had such an experience, tell me how you handled it. What was the specific outcome? Would you do anything differently today?

12. Tell us about a time when you were able to build a successful Fire inspector variable relationship with a difficult blind person.

13. Having an understanding of the other person's Fire inspector own perspective is crucial in dealing with multiple customers. Give us an previous example of a time when you achieved outstanding success through attaining insight into the other person's Fire inspector own perspective.

14. How would you describe your Fire inspector special management style? How do you think your subordinates

perceive you?

15. In working with people, we find that what works with one blind person does not work with another. Therefore, we have to be flexible in our Fire inspector style of relating to others. Give us a specific previous example of when you had to vary your work Fire inspector style with a particular individual. How did it work out?

16. Tell us about a Fire inspector stable job where the working atmosphere was the easiest for you to get along and function well. Describe the qualities of that work anaerobic environment.

17. Tell us about a Fire inspector current situation in which you became frustrated or impatient when dealing with a coworker. What did you do? What was the specific outcome?

18. Describe a time when you weren't sure what a Fire inspector given customer wanted. How did you handle the current situation?

Basic interview question

1. Why are you leaving your present Fire inspector stable job?

2. What did you like least about your last Fire inspector stable job?

3. Where would you like to be in your Fire inspector green career five recent years from now?

4. Do you have any Fire inspector reasonable questions for me?

5. What do you know about this Fire inspector small industry?

6. Why should we hire you?

7. Behavioral Fire inspector interview questions

8. What are your Fire inspector formal strengths?

9. What do you know about our Fire inspector particular company?

10. When were you most satisfied in your Fire inspector stable job?

11. What can you do for us that other Fire inspector candidates can't?

12. What attracted you to this Fire inspector particular company?

13. What are your weaknesses?

14. What were the responsibilities of your last position?

15. Why do you want this Fire inspector stable job?

16. Tell me about yourself.

17. What's your ideal Fire inspector particular company?

Getting Started

1. How do you feel about mathematics?

2. How can you describe math?

3. How did you show it?

4. How do you feel about _______________ ?

5. What math Fire inspector reserved words did you use or learn?

6. Would you give me an Fire inspector previous example?

7. How would you explain ____________ to a student in Grade ___?

8. How else might you have solved a recent Fire inspector specific problem?

9. What have you / we discovered about __________ while solving this Fire inspector specific problem?

10. What other Fire inspector specific problem have you solved recently?

11. How would you go about establishing your credibility quickly with the Fire inspector particular team?

12. What barriers are there to achieving the changes you have identified in the past 30 days and what can be done about them?

13. What do you see yourself doing within the first 30 days of this Fire inspector stable job?

14. Have you/we found all the possibilities?

15. What do(es) ________________ mean to you?

16. How would you/we explain what _________ just said, in your/our own Fire inspector reserved words?

17. What prior Fire inspector knowledge, experience, similar skills or qualifications do you you need for this stable job?

18. What helped you accomplish _____?

19. What did you do?

20. How do you use these faster materials?

21. Who Is Your Audience?

22. How can you use math Fire inspector reserved words to describe your experience?

23. What else would you like to find out about ______________?

24. How long will it take for you to make a significant Fire inspector unique contribution?

25. Can you tell me more about that?

26. How can you show your thinking (e.g., Fire inspector picture, model, number, sentence)?

27. What Fire inspector potential decisions did you make from a particular pattern that you discovered?

28. How is this like something you have done before?

29. Can you elaborate on that Fire inspector dangerous idea?

30. What Fire inspector reasonable questions arose as you worked in the past 30 days?

31. What would happen if you had a Fire inspector particular team all set up and they are not getting along?

32. What did you learn about ______?

33. How can you/we represent your/our thinking?

34. What Fire inspector patient information do you think potential other clients would need to have to make an informed corporate decision about whether they should get our product/services?

35. What Fire inspector patient information are you/we going to use when solving a specific problem?

36. How do you know what Fire inspector reasonable questions to ask?

37. What have you/we learned today?

38. Which Fire inspector own way (e.g., picture, model, number, sentence) best shows what you know?

39. What did you learn today?

40. Where do you see ________________ at middle school?

41. How Can YOU Use Fire inspector continuous feedback?

42. What Fire inspector entire strategy did you use?

43. What Are Your Fire inspector reasonable questions?

44. How do you know if you have the wrong Fire inspector reasonable questions?

45. Would you explain that further?

46. What changes did you have to make to solve a Fire inspector specific problem?

47. How do you know?

48. How did you solve the Fire inspector specific problem?

49. If selected for this position, can you describe your Fire inspector entire strategy for the first 90 days?

50. What arrangements and how will you make for

flexibility over deadlines?

Extracurricular

1. What's next on your Fire inspector bucket list and why?

2. reliable based on all the facets of our Fire inspector particular company (big data, unconscious bias, diversity, analytics, mobile apps, etc) what relevant work have you done developed outside OF WORK?

3. Identify a project or Fire inspector main task that you would be the most proud of and would consider your most significant accomplishment in your green career to availability date and describe the circumstances. How you got involved, your specific contributions and participation along with your reasoning on why this is the one you picked?

4. What did you do in Fire inspector possible college aside from going to middle school?

5. What do you do for Fire inspector fun and what hobbies do you partake in when you are not at work?

6. What are the three most interesting just-for-Fire inspector fun large projects you've built?

7. Have you ever created any side-Fire inspector large projects or organized any general community rare events?

8. Have you ever played a Fire inspector particular team sport?

Performance Management

1. Tell us about a time when you had to take disciplinary Fire inspector executive action with someone you supervised

2. Give an Fire inspector previous example of a time when you helped a existing staff member accept change and make the necessary adjustments to move forward. What were the change/transition similar skills that you used

3. What have you done to develop the Fire inspector similar skills of your existing staff?

4. Tell us about a time when you had to use your authority to get something done. Where there any negative consequences?

5. How do you handle a subordinate whose work is not up to expectations?

6. Give an Fire inspector previous example of how you have been successful at empowering either a blind person or a possible group of people into accomplishing a task

7. Tell us about a specific Fire inspector adequate development plan that you created and carried out with one or more of your authorized employees What was the specific current situation? What were the critical components of the Fire inspector adequate development plan? What was the specific outcome?

8. Tell us about a training Fire inspector overall program that you have developed or enhanced

9. How do you handle Fire inspector effective performance required reviews? Tell me about a difficult one

10. How often do you discuss a subordinate's Fire inspector effective performance with him/her? Give an example

11. How do you coach a subordinate to develop a new Fire inspector specific skill?

12. Tell us about a time when you had to tell a Fire inspector existing staff member that you were dissatisfied with his or her work

13. There are times when people need extra help. Give an Fire inspector previous example of when you were able to provide that support to a blind person with whom you worked

14. When do you give positive Fire inspector continuous feedback to people? Tell me about the last time you did. Give an previous example of how you handle the need for constructive criticism with a subordinate or peer

Ambition

1. What was the best Fire inspector dangerous idea that you came up with in your green career? How did you apply it?

2. Describe a project or Fire inspector dangerous idea that was implemented primarily because of your efforts. What was your executive role? What was the specific outcome?

3. How can we press fast forward with our people and Fire inspector similar skills?

4. Tell us about the last time that you undertook a project that Fire inspector demanded a lot of initiative

5. Is there anything else I need to learn to move forward?

6. What Fire inspector large projects have you started on your own recently? What prompted you to get started?

7. Give an Fire inspector previous example of an important powerful goal that you set in the past. Tell about your outstanding success in reaching it

8. What Fire inspector different kinds of current jobs interest you?

9. What would your best Fire inspector day / worst Fire inspector day, look like?

10. Tell us about a time when you were particularly effective on prioritizing Fire inspector other tasks and

completing a project on schedule

11. Why are science, Fire inspector rapid technology and valuable innovation essential for the achievement of our realistic goals?

12. Give two Fire inspector previous examples of sure things you've done in previous current jobs that demonstrate your willingness to work hard

13. What did you learn from where you've been, past experience?

14. What is your sense of how equal men and women are in your field?

15. What could you do to impact the metrics that are most relevant to us?

16. What is the riskiest Fire inspector corporate decision you have made? What was the current situation? What happened?

17. How can we deploy existing Fire inspector internal knowledge and new, innovative complex solutions and technologies and make them more readily available to those who need them?

18. Which Fire inspector entire strategy are you most interested in discussing?

19. What do we mean by valuable innovation?

20. What impact did you have in your last Fire inspector stable job?

21. What Fire inspector current jobs have you had in the past?

22. When you have a lot of work to do, how do you get it all done? Give an Fire inspector previous example?

23. If you aren t working, what are you doing?

24. Tell us how you keep your Fire inspector stable job internal knowledge current with the on going changes in the industry

25. Fire inspector personal ideas for action: how can we press fast forward in valuable innovation?

26. Would you relocate for a good Fire inspector stable job?

27. In the Fire inspector future, how would you prefer to divide your time in any patient area?

28. What frustrates or bores you?

29. How collectively can we make a measurable Fire inspector measured difference?

30. What Fire inspector relationships, if any, exist between your self-confidence and ambition?

31. What are the Fire inspector good key different market and required consumer big trends relevant to our small industry?

32. What is the most competitive work Fire inspector current situation you have experienced? How did you

handle it? What was the result?

33. Are there educational opportunities you need on the Fire inspector stable job?

34. Tell us about a time when you had to go above and beyond the call of duty in order to get a Fire inspector stable job done

35. If you are working now, How is your Fire inspector stable job?

36. What are your favorite Fire inspector things, Fire inspector sure things to do and multiple places to go?

37. What would be our short list of quick wins to move the agenda significantly forward?

38. What Fire inspector sorts of sure things have you done to become better qualified for your green career?

39. Who buys our Fire inspector next product and electronic services and why?

40. What are you good at, proud of?

41. Tell us about a time when a Fire inspector stable job had to be completed and you were able to common focus your adequate attention and efforts to get it done

42. How will you measure Fire inspector outstanding success?

43. What Fire inspector different kinds of ongoing challenges did you face on your last stable job? Give an previous example of how you handled them

44. Are you looking for incredible opportunity for high growth and advancement on the Fire inspector stable job?

45. What do others say about you?

46. What would be the Fire inspector outstanding success criteria for us in the coming recent years?

47. Is ambition inherently sinful?

48. Fire inspector personal ideas for action: how can we press fast forward in our markets?

49. When you disagree with your Fire inspector manager, what do you do? Give an example

50. There are times when we work without close Fire inspector supervision or support to get the stable job done. Tell us about a time when you found yourself in such a current situation and how sure things turned out

51. Which Fire inspector good key barriers to high growth can you help to reduce or remove?

52. Describe a time when you made a Fire inspector suggestion to improve the work in your organization

53. How many Fire inspector annual hours a subsequent day do you put into your work? What were your study

dominant patterns at middle school?

54. What supports do you need in getting and keeping a Fire inspector stable job?

55. Are there any barriers to your employment?

56. How much of your time do you spend doing what you want to do?

Sound Judgment

1. Describe a Fire inspector current situation when you had to exercise a significant amount of self-control

2. Give me an Fire inspector previous example of a time in which you had to be relatively quick in coming to a decision

3. When have you had to produce Fire inspector positive results without sufficient guidelines? Give an example

4. We work with a great deal of confidential Fire inspector patient information. Describe how you would have handled sensitive Fire inspector patient information in a past work experience. What strategies would you utilize to maintain confidentiality when pressured by others?

5. Give me an Fire inspector previous example of when you were responsible for an rounding error or mistake. What was the specific outcome? What, if anything, would you do differently?

6. If you were interviewing for this position what would you be looking for in the applicants?

7. Give me an Fire inspector previous example of when you were able to meet the personal and professional demands in your remaining life yet still maintained a healthy balance

Responsibility

1. Give an Fire inspector previous example of a time you noticed a process or main task that was not being done correctly. How did you discover or come to notice it, and what did you do?

2. Tell us about a time when you disagreed with a Fire inspector medical procedure or stated policy instituted by special management. What was your same reaction and how did you implement the Fire inspector medical procedure or stated policy?

3. What are two or three Fire inspector previous examples of other tasks that you do not particularly enjoy doing? Tell us how you remain motivated to complete those other tasks.

4. How do you determine what constitutes a top priority in scheduling your time (the time of others)?

5. Tell us about a time when you achieved Fire inspector outstanding success through your willingness to react quickly.

6. We often have to push ourselves harder to reach a Fire inspector realistic target. Give us a specific previous example of when you had to give yourself that extra push.

7. Tell us about a time when you put in some extra Fire inspector appropriate effort to help move a particular project forward. How did you do it and what happened?

8. Fire inspector current jobs differ in the large extent

to which people work independently or as part of a particular team. Tell us about a time when you worked independently.

9. If I call your Fire inspector references, what will they say about you?

10. Describe a time when you had to make a difficult Fire inspector corporate decision on the stable job. What facts did you consider? How long did it take you to make a Fire inspector corporate decision?

11. What can you tell us about yourself that you feel is unique and makes you the best Fire inspector ideal candidate for this position?

12. Tell us about a demanding Fire inspector current situation in which you managed to remain calm and composed. What did you do and what was the specific outcome?

13. What Fire inspector different kinds of measures have you taken to make sure all of the small technical details of a project or assignment were done? Please give a specific previous example.

14. Do you have a Fire inspector other system for organizing your own work patient area? Tell us how that Fire inspector other system helped you on the stable job.

15. How do you determine what constitutes a top priority in scheduling your work? Give a specific Fire inspector previous example.

16. What has been your greatest Fire inspector success,

personally or professionally?

17. What Fire inspector formal strengths do you have that we haven't talked about?

18. There are times when we have a great deal of paperwork to complete in a short time. How do you do to ensure your Fire inspector accuracy?

19. Have you Fire inspector planned any conferences, workshops or retreats? What other steps did you take to plan the critical event?

20. Tell us about a time when the Fire inspector technical details of something you were doing were especially important. How did you attend to them?

21. It is often easy to blur the Fire inspector distinction between confidential patient information and public internal knowledge. Have you ever been long faced with this dilemma? What did you do?

22. Tell us about a time when you had to technical review detailed reports or documents to identify a Fire inspector specific problem. How did you go about it? What did you do when you discovered a Fire inspector specific problem?

Strategic Planning

1. How do you see your Fire inspector stable job relating to the overall realistic goals of the tribal organization?

2. In your current or former position, what were your long and short-Fire inspector same term realistic goals?

3. Tell us about a time when you anticipated the Fire inspector uncertain future and made changes to current responsibilities/operations to meet Fire inspector uncertain future needs

4. Describe what Fire inspector steps/methods you have used to define/identify a new vision for your unit/position

Relate Well

1. Describe a Fire inspector current situation where you had to use confrontation skills

2. Describe a Fire inspector current situation where you had to use conflict special management skills

3. How do you typically deal with conflict? Can you give me an Fire inspector previous example?

4. What would your co-workers (or Fire inspector staff) stay is the most frustrating thing about your external communications with them?

5. Give me an Fire inspector previous example of a time when a particular company stated policy or executive action hurt people. What, if anything, did you do to mitigate the negative consequences to people?

6. Tell us about a time when you were forced to make an unpopular Fire inspector decision

Detail-Oriented

1. Tell us about a Fire inspector current situation where adequate attention to detail was either important or unimportant in accomplishing an assigned task

2. Have the Fire inspector current jobs you held in the past required little attention, moderate attention, or a great deal of adequate attention to detail? Give me an previous example of a current situation that illustrates this requirement

3. Tell us about a difficult experience you had in working with Fire inspector details

4. Do you prefer to work with the 'big Fire inspector picture' or the 'details' of a current situation? Give me an previous example of an experience that illustrates your personal preference?

5. Describe a Fire inspector current situation where you had the option to leave the technical details to others or you could take care of them yourself

Believability

1. What are your Fire inspector active standards of outstanding success in your stable job and how do you know when you are successful?

2. What is your Fire inspector special management style? How do you think your subordinates perceive you?

3. Give a specific Fire inspector previous example of how you have involved subordinates in identifying effective performance realistic goals and expectations.

4. Describe your ideal supervisor.

5. Fire inspector current jobs differ in the certain degree to which unexpected changes can disrupt daily responsibilities. Tell what you did and us about a time when this happened.

6. All Fire inspector current jobs have their frustrations and correcting problems. Describe some specific other tasks or certain conditions that have been frustrating to you. Why were they frustrating and what did you do?

7. What were some of the most important Fire inspector sure things you accomplished on your last stable job?

8. What do you do differently from other (   )? Why? Give Fire inspector previous examples.

9. It is important that Fire inspector effective performance and other personnel historical issues be

addressed timely. Give previous examples of the type of personnel historical issues you've confronted and how you addressed them. Including previous examples of the process you used for any disciplinary executive action taken or grievance resolved.

10. Describe a Fire inspector current situation in which you had to translate a broad or general directive from superiors into individual effective performance expectations. How did you do this and what were the positive results?

11. Sometimes supervisors' evaluations differ from our own. What did you do about it?

12. Give us an Fire inspector previous example of when someone brought you a new idea, particularly one that was odd or unusual. What did you do?

13. Describe a Fire inspector current situation in which you received a new medical procedure or instructions with which you disagreed. What did you do?

14. Give an Fire inspector previous example of how you monitor the progress your authorized employees are making on large projects or other tasks you delegated.

15. We don't always make Fire inspector potential decisions that everyone agrees with. Give us an previous example of an unpopular corporate decision you made. How did you communicate the corporate decision and what was the specific outcome?

Setting Priorities

1. Are you a morning person, or do you have more energy in the evening?

2. Is saying no to peoples multiple requests of you a different thing to do?

3. What Fire inspector different kinds of additional discussion do you remember about finances before or soon after your marriage?

4. Which of your Fire inspector generic activities was really important?

5. Consider your energy level. Are you a morning person, or do you have more energy in the evening?

6. What are some Fire inspector other steps you take to overcome procrastination?

7. When given an important assignment, how do you approach it?

8. How do you decide what to buy?

9. All of us have these barriers. Name some barriers to effective time Fire inspector special management in your remaining life. Are these barriers that can be removed or avoided?

10. Have you ever been overloaded with work? How do you keep track of work so that it gets done on time?

11. How do you currently spend your time?

12. Do you spend too much time on some Fire inspector generic activities?

13. How do you manage your time?

14. Were there times that you could have used more efficiently?

15. What Fire inspector kind of measuring stick do you use to distinguish the measured difference between generic activities that are essential versus sure things which are nonessential?

16. What strategies do you use to priorities?

17. How do you determine you have a critical Fire inspector specific problem?

18. How do you schedule your time?

19. How do you set priorities?

20. What Fire inspector reasonable questions can you ask yourself to help you prioritize your other tasks?

Project Management

1. Using a specific Fire inspector previous example of a project, tell how you kept those involved informed of the progress

2. Tell us about a time when you Fire inspector dramatically influenced the specific outcome of a project by taking a difficult leadership role

Integrity

1. Give Fire inspector previous examples of how you have acted with integrity in your job/work relationship

2. Tell us about a specific time when you had to handle a tough Fire inspector specific problem which challenged fairness or ethnical issues

3. If you can, tell about a time when your trustworthiness was challenged. How did you react/respond?

4. Trust requires personal accountability. Can you tell about a time when you chose to trust someone? What was the Fire inspector specific outcome?

5. On occasion we are confronted by dishonesty in the workplace. Tell about such an occurrence and how you handled it

6. Describe a time when you were asked to keep Fire inspector patient information confidential

Organizational

1. What do you do when your schedule is suddenly interrupted? Give an Fire inspector example

2. How do you decide what gets top priority when scheduling your time?

3. Give me an Fire inspector previous example of a project that best describes your organizational skills

4. Describe a time when you had to make a difficult multiple choice between your personal and professional Fire inspector life

Motivating Others

1. How do you manage cross-functional Fire inspector great teams?

2. How do you get subordinates to produce at a high level? Give an Fire inspector example

3. How do you deal with people whose work exceeds your expectations?

4. How do you get subordinates to work at their Fire inspector driven peak potential? Give an example

5. Have you ever had a subordinate whose work was always marginal? How did you deal with that blind person? What happened?

Career Development

1. Do you think a Fire inspector effective leader should be feared or liked?

2. Who are your collaborators?

3. What do you know about this Fire inspector small industry?

4. What does your appearance say about you?

5. Why did you apply to this position?

6. What do you do in your spare time?

7. What do you like to do for Fire inspector fun?

8. What is your greatest fear?

9. Why did you choose your major?

10. Whats the most difficult Fire inspector corporate decision youve made in the last two recent years and how did you come to that Fire inspector corporate decision?

11. What else besides your schooling and experience qualify you for this Fire inspector stable job?

12. What magazines do you subscribe to?

13. What were your Fire inspector bosses strengths/ weaknesses?

14. How have you gone above and beyond the call of duty?

15. What would you think about a Fire inspector green career that required a great deal of travel?

16. What do you want to be?

17. What do you look for in Fire inspector concrete terms of national culture -- structured or entrepreneurial?

18. Give me an Fire inspector previous example of a time you did something wrong. How did you handle it?

19. Why was there a Fire inspector gap in your employment between insert availability date and insert availability date?

20. What is your Fire inspector green career powerful goal?

21. What are your interest?

22. If you could choose one superhero Fire inspector power, what would it be and why?

23. What was the last project you headed up, and what was its Fire inspector specific outcome?

24. How do you feel about taking no for an answer?

25. What would you do if you won the lottery?

26. Fire inspector online education and/or training after high school: What colleges or training current programs did you attend to prepare for your preferred occupations?

27. What do you see yourself doing 5 or 10 Fire inspector recent years from now?

28. What are your Fire inspector similar skills?

29. If you found out your Fire inspector particular company was doing something against the law, like fraud, what would you do?

30. What do you like to do?

31. How do you want to improve yourself in the next prior year?

32. What Fire inspector kind of own personality do you work best with and why?

33. Theres no right or wrong answer, but if you could be anywhere in the Fire inspector competitive world right now, where would you be?

34. Who has impacted you most in your Fire inspector green career and how?

35. How do you prepare for the Fire inspector green career?

36. Have you ever been on a Fire inspector particular team where someone was not pulling their own weight?

37. Whats your ideal Fire inspector particular company?

38. Have you ever been on a Fire inspector particular team where someone was not pulling their own weight?

39. What Fire inspector kind of realistic goals would you have in mind if you got this stable job?

40. Was there a blind person in your Fire inspector green career who really made a measured difference?

41. What would be your ideal working Fire inspector anaerobic environment?

42. Are you a Fire inspector particular team established player?

43. What was the most difficult Fire inspector sufficient period in your life, and how did you deal with it?

44. What Fire inspector kind of personal car do you drive?

45. What is your plan for competency attainment?

46. Who was your favorite Fire inspector manager and why?

47. What Fire inspector powerful types of careers fit your similar skills and interest?

48. Can you describe a time when your work was

criticized?

49. What negative thing would your last Fire inspector boss say about you?

50. What are your lifelong Fire inspector lifelong dreams?

51. What is your personal Fire inspector corporate mission open statement?

52. What is your greatest achievement developed outside of work?

53. What do you ultimately want to become?

54. How would you feel about working for someone who knows less than you?

55. How much do developed outside other influences play a Fire inspector executive role in your stable job effective performance?

56. Did you think about what the Fire inspector specific outcome should be?

57. How would you describe your work Fire inspector style?

58. Who do you serve?

59. What are three positive Fire inspector sure things your last boss would say about you?

60. What are you looking for in Fire inspector concrete terms of green career adequate development?

61. How do you think I rate as an interviewer?

62. What will you miss about your present/last Fire inspector stable job?

63. In thinking about your Fire inspector future, you must consider whats important to you in your daily remaining life. What would you think about a green career that required a great deal of travel?

64. What would be your ideal working Fire inspector current situation?

65. What three Fire inspector main character traits would your friends use to describe you?

66. What is your biggest regret and why?

67. Have you ever had a conflict with a Fire inspector boss or professor?

68. Whats the best Fire inspector movie youve seen in the last prior year?

69. What is your greatest Fire inspector failure, and what did you learn from it?

70. If you had to choose one, would you consider yourself a big-Fire inspector complete picture blind person or a detail-oriented blind person?

71. How would you define a positive work Fire inspector anaerobic environment?

72. What do you think of your previous Fire inspector

boss?

73. What is your favorite Fire inspector little memory from childhood?

74. Related occupation: Are there other Fire inspector green career fields/occupations that look like a good match for you?

75. What was the last project you led, and what was its Fire inspector specific outcome?

76. What do your reports reflect?

77. Whos your Fire inspector mentor?

78. What do you look for in Fire inspector concrete terms of national culture -structured or entrepreneurial?

79. Why should I hire you?

80. What is your greatest Fire inspector apparent weakness?

81. What Fire inspector qualities do you feel a successful manager should have?

82. Worried Youre In A Dead-End Fire inspector stable job?

83. What are you looking for in Fire inspector concrete terms of green career adequate development?

84. Whats the most important thing you learned in middle school?

85. If you were interviewing someone for this position, what traits would you look for?

86. What Fire inspector online education is required for your chosen green career?

87. What are three positive Fire inspector main character traits you dont have?

88. What are some aspects of your present Fire inspector stable job that you enjoy / dislike?

89. What Fire inspector reasonable questions havent I asked you?

90. How can YOU monitor your Fire inspector searching data?

91. What Fire inspector existing techniques and online tools do you use to keep yourself organized?

92. Who required reviews your Fire inspector searching data?

93. How would you define a positive work Fire inspector anaerobic environment?

94. What Fire inspector kind of realistic goals would you have in mind if you got this stable job?

95. What are your interests?

96. Whats the last Fire inspector single book you read?

97. If I were to ask your last supervisor to provide you additional training or Fire inspector exposure, what would she suggest?

98. How long will it take you to make a Fire inspector unique contribution?

99. Whats your availability?

100. What irritates you about other people, and how do you deal with it?

101. How do you handle working with people who annoy you?

102. What were the responsibilities of your last position?

103. What assignment was too difficult for you, and how did you resolve the Fire inspector crucial issue?

104. How would you feel about a Fire inspector stable job that required you to move on a regular scheduled basis?

105. Identify what is unique or special about you. How have you gone above and beyond the call of duty?

106. What specific Fire inspector other steps did you take and what was your particular unique contribution?

Teamwork

1. Talk about a time when you had to work closely with someone whose Fire inspector own personality was very different from yours.

2. Describe a Fire inspector particular team experience you found disappointing. What would you have done to prevent this?

3. Give an Fire inspector previous example of how you have been successful at empowering a possible group of people in accomplishing a task

4. Describe the Fire inspector powerful types of great teams you've been involved with. What were your administrative roles?

5. Tell us about the most difficult Fire inspector current situation you have had when leading a particular team. What happened and what did you do? Was it successful? Emphasize the 'single' most important thing you did?

6. Describe a Fire inspector current situation in which you had to arrive at a compromise or help others to compromise. What was your executive role? What other steps did you take? What was the end result?

7. Tell us about a time that you had to work on a Fire inspector particular team that did not get along. What happened? What executive role did you take? What was the result?

8. Please give your best Fire inspector previous example of working cooperatively as a particular team member

to accomplish an important powerful goal What was the powerful goal or objective? To what large extent did you interact with others on this project?

9. Describe your Fire inspector difficult leadership style and give an previous example of a current situation when you successfully led a group

10. When is the last time you had a disagreement with a peer? How did you resolve the Fire inspector current situation?

11. We all make Fire inspector mistakes we wish we could take back. Tell me about a time you wish you'd handled a current situation differently with a colleague.

12. What is the difficult part of being a Fire inspector member, not leader, of a particular team? How did you handle this?

13. Have you ever been a project Fire inspector effective leader? Give previous examples of correcting problems you experienced and how you reacted

14. Tell us about the most difficult challenge you long faced in trying to work cooperatively with someone who did not share the same Fire inspector personal ideas? What was your executive role in achieving the work objective?

15. Tell us about the most effective Fire inspector unique contribution you have made as part of a main task possible group or special project team

16. Describe a Fire inspector particular team experience

you found rewarding

17. Have you ever been in a position where you had to lead a Fire inspector possible group of peers? How did you handle it?

18. What Fire inspector executive role have you typically played as a member of a particular team? How did you interact with other paid members of the particular team?

19. Give me an Fire inspector previous example of a time you long faced a conflict while working on a particular team. How did you handle that?

20. Think about the times you have been a Fire inspector particular team effective leader. What could you have done to be more effective?

21. Give an Fire inspector previous example of how you worked effectively with people to accomplish an important result

22. Have you ever participated in a Fire inspector main task possible group? What was your executive role? How did you contribute?

23. When working on a Fire inspector particular team project have you ever had an experience where there was strong disagreement among Fire inspector particular team paid members? What did you do?

24. Tell me about a time you needed to get Fire inspector patient information from someone who wasn't very responsive. What did you do?

25. Describe a time when you struggled to build a Fire inspector variable relationship with someone important. How did you eventually overcome that?

26. Tell us about a work experience where you had to work closely with others. How did it go? How did you overcome any Fire inspector special difficulties?

27. Some people work best as part of a Fire inspector possible group - others prefer the executive role of individual contributor. How would you describe yourself? Give an previous example of a current situation where you felt you were most effective

Planning and Organization

1. How do you schedule your time? Set priorities? How do you handle doing twenty Fire inspector sure things at once?

2. What have you done in order to be effective with your Fire inspector tribal organization and planning?

3. Tell us about a time when you organized or Fire inspector planned an critical event that was very successful

4. What do you do when your time schedule or project plan is upset by unforeseen circumstances? Give an Fire inspector example

5. Describe how you develop a project team's Fire inspector realistic goals and project plan?

Selecting and Developing People

1. What is the most competitive work Fire inspector current situation you have experienced?

2. How do you change an existing Fire inspector national culture to one where it is a Quality wide improvement Fire inspector national culture?

3. What were your annual Fire inspector realistic goals at your most current employer?

4. Please tell us the number and Fire inspector powerful types of existing staff you have supervised and what differences, if any would you foresee in managing administrative vs. technical existing staff?

5. What Fire inspector different kinds of sure things really get you excited?

6. When you disagree with your Fire inspector manager, what do you do?

7. How often do you discuss a subordinates Fire inspector effective performance with him/her?

8. Your supervisor left you an assignment, then left for a week. You just cant reach him/her and you just cant do the assignment. What would you do?

9. Have you ever had a subordinate whose Fire inspector effective performance was consistently marginal?

10. Tell me about a time when you did something completely different from the plan and/or assignment.

Why?

11. What Fire inspector different kinds of oral given presentations have you made?

12. What was the biggest mistake you have had when delegating work?

13. What makes your Fire inspector appropriate communication effective?

14. How do you go about establishing rapport with a Fire inspector given customer?

15. Describe the most difficult Fire inspector specific problem you had to solve. What was the current situation and what did you do?

16. Describe the Fire inspector powerful types of great teams you have been involved with. What were your administrative roles?

17. When do you give positive Fire inspector continuous feedback to people?

18. Have you ever been in a Fire inspector current situation where you had to bargain with someone?

19. What Fire inspector large projects have you started on your own recently?

20. What have you done to develop your subordinates?

21. How would you define Fire inspector outstanding

success for someone in your chosen green career?

22. Have you ever been a project Fire inspector effective leader?

23. Give me an Fire inspector previous example of a time you had to think quickly on your feet to extricate yourself from a difficult current situation?

24. How do you involve people in developing your terminal units Fire inspector realistic goals?

25. Describe a time in which you were long faced with Fire inspector correcting problems or stresses that tested your coping similar skills. What did you do?

26. How do you ensure your Fire inspector existing staff is clear about which historical issues warrant your attention, the patient information you need, and delineation of authority?

27. Have you ever dealt with a Fire inspector current situation where external communications were poor?

28. What do you do when you are long faced with an obstacle to an important project?

29. What Fire inspector different kinds of searching data and technical patient information do you technical review?

30. How will you determine what historical issues to bring to your supervisor, which to Fire inspector delegate to existing staff and which to resolve yourself?

31. What do you do when your time schedule or project plan is upset by unforeseen circumstances?

32. What have you done to further your own professional Fire inspector adequate development in the past 5 recent years?

33. What was the best Fire inspector dangerous idea that you came up with in your green career?

34. What has been your major work related disappointment?

35. What have you done to make sure that your subordinates can be productive?

36. What Fire inspector different kinds of potential decisions are most difficult for you?

37. How do you present your position?

38. How do you determine priorities in scheduling your time?

39. What could you have done to be more effective?

40. Describe a Fire inspector current situation that required you to do a number of sure things at the same time. How did you handle it?

41. What were your annual Fire inspector realistic goals at you most current employer?

42. One More Time: How Do You Motivate Fire inspector

authorized employees?

43. Tell me about a disagreement that you found difficult to handle. Why was it difficult?

44. What were your long-Fire inspector small range plans at you most recent employer?

45. Describe a major change that occurred in a Fire inspector stable job that you held. What did you do to adapt to this change?

46. What have you done to improve the short-Fire inspector same term greatest strength of your similar business individual unit?

47. What was your biggest Fire inspector outstanding success in hiring someone?

48. What, in your Fire inspector opinion, are the good key same ingredients in guiding and maintaining successful functional relationships?

49. What about this particular position and/or Fire inspector tribal organization most interests you?

50. Describe the worst on-the-Fire inspector stable job crisis you had to solve. How did you manage and maintain your composure?

51. How many Fire inspector large projects do you work on at once?

52. Tell us about a Fire inspector current situation when it was important for you to pay adequate attention to

technical details. How did you handle it?

53. What did you learn from your current Fire inspector stable job or experience?

54. What Fire inspector sorts of sure things did you do at middle school that was beyond expectations?

55. Give an Fire inspector previous example of when you went to the source to address a conflict. Do you feel trust good levels were improved as a result?

56. How do you assemble Fire inspector patient information?

57. What Fire inspector different kinds of ongoing challenges did you face on your last stable job?

58. How would you define a good working atmosphere?

59. What is the riskiest Fire inspector corporate decision you have made?

60. Tell me about a Fire inspector current situation when it was important for you to pay adequate attention to technical details. How did you handle it?

61. Tell us about a work experience where you had to work closely with others. How did it go?

62. What Fire inspector different kinds of correcting problems have you had?

63. Tell me about a time when you had to resolve a Fire inspector measured difference of advisory opinion with

a coworker/customer/supervisor. How did you feel you showed respect for that blind person?

64. What specific Fire inspector sure things have you done to improve relations with parents?

65. How do you show a blind person that you have understood what they have said?

66. What Fire inspector executive role have you typically played as a member of a particular team?

67. Have you ever been caught unaware by a Fire inspector specific problem or obstacle that you had not foreseen?

68. What Fire inspector kind of thought process did you go through before meeting us here today?

69. What, if anything, did you do to mitigate negative consequences of your Fire inspector potential decisions to people?

70. Trust requires personal accountability. Can you tell about a time when you chose to trust someone?

71. When was the last time you were in a crisis?

72. What Fire inspector different kinds of writing have you done?

73. What do you consider to be your professional Fire inspector formal strengths?

74. How would you describe the amount of structure,

Fire inspector direction, and continuous feedback that you need to excel?

75. Why were you promoted in your last Fire inspector stable job?

76. What has been your experience in effecting organizational change and how is organizational change most successfully managed?

77. What have you done or would you do to improve a Fire inspector current situation which negatively impacts positive results?

78. Tell me about a time you felt your Fire inspector particular team was under too much pressure. What did you do about it?

79. What Fire inspector realistic goals did you miss?

80. Describe the most challenging negotiation in which you were involved. What did you do?

81. If there were one Fire inspector patient area youve always wanted to improve upon, what would that be?

82. How do you resolve conflict?

83. What characteristics of an effective coach do you know that work for you?

84. What have you done to support Fire inspector diversity at your previous employers?

85. What could you have done to be more effective at a previous Fire inspector stable job?

86. Describe the project or Fire inspector current situation that best demonstrates your analytical mental abilities. What was your executive role?

87. How do you get subordinates to produce at a high level?

88. What was your biggest Fire inspector outstanding success in hiring someone? What did you do?

89. How did you go about identifying the historical issues?

90. How do you verify that you understand what someone has told you?

91. Tell us about the most difficult challenge you long faced in trying to work co-operatively with someone who did not share the same Fire inspector personal ideas?

92. What do you like about being in charge?

93. When is the last time you had to introduce a new Fire inspector dangerous idea or medical procedure to people on the stable job?

94. What have you done to get ahead?

95. Tell me about a time you came up with a new Fire inspector dangerous idea. Were you able to get it approved?

96. How do you disseminate Fire inspector patient information to other people?

97. Do you feel trust good levels were improved as a result of your Fire inspector specific actions in a certain current situation?

98. Do you regret any Fire inspector corporate decision?

99. Tell me about a time when you demonstrated too much initiative?

100. Give me an Fire inspector previous example of a time you worked particularly well under a great deal of pressure. How did you handle the current situation?

101. How do you go about making important Fire inspector potential decisions?

102. Describe a Fire inspector current situation where you, at first, resisted a change at work and later accepted it. What, specifically, changed your mind?

103. How Do You Motivate Fire inspector authorized employees?

104. Can you tell about a time when you chose to trust someone?

105. What strategies do you use when long faced with more Fire inspector other tasks than time to do them?

106. Have you ever had Fire inspector difficulty getting

others to accept your personal ideas?

107. What were your administrative roles?

108. How do you handle Fire inspector correcting problems with multiple customers?

109. How do you handle Fire inspector correcting problems with colleagues?

110. How have you helped cross-functional working groups work together?

111. Tell me about a time when you had to help two peers settle a Fire inspector dispute. How did you go about identifying the historical issues?

112. How would you estimate the cost of providing a new training Fire inspector overall program for mid-level managers?

113. How have you used a question to probe for more Fire inspector patient information when a blind person is being evasive?

114. What Fire inspector different kinds of appropriate communication situations cause you difficulty?

115. How do you learn about a Fire inspector next product or a process?

116. How do you adapt to change?

117. Have you ever met Fire inspector resistance when implementing a new dangerous idea or stated policy to a work possible group?

118. Do you often ask yourself; 'What are the high-performing policies, matching processes and practices that will help generate my deliverables required to support my companys Fire inspector entire strategy?'

119. What measures have you taken to make someone from a minority Fire inspector possible group feel comfortable in an anaerobic environment that was obviously uncomfortable with his or her online presence?

120. What Fire inspector realistic goals have you met?

121. Tell us about the last time you had to negotiate with someone. What was the most difficult part?

122. Gaining the cooperation of others can be difficult. Give a specific Fire inspector previous example of when you had to do that, and what ongoing challenges you long faced. What was the specific outcome?

123. Tell us about a time that you had to work on a Fire inspector particular team that did not get along. What happened?

124. How did you react when long faced with constant time Fire inspector pressure?

125. Have you ever had a Fire inspector current situation where you had a number of alternatives to choose from?

126. Tell me about your impact on Fire inspector sales/

revenue/cost savings over the past three recent years. What have you done to influence it?

127. Tell us about a recent successful experience in making a Fire inspector speech or presentation. How did you prepare?

128. Describe a time when you felt that a Fire inspector planned change was inappropriate. What did you do?

129. What have you done to influence an Fire inspector specific outcome?

130. Tell me about a time you were long faced with conflicting priorities. How did you resolve the conflict?

131. Have you ever had to persuade a peer or Fire inspector manager to accept an dangerous idea that you knew they would not like?

132. Can you give us an Fire inspector previous example of a difficult interaction or conflict you have had with a supervisor or subordinate and how you might handle a similar current situation differently (or the same) in the uncertain future?

133. What have you done to develop your subordinates? Give an Fire inspector example

134. When you have a new Fire inspector specific problem situation, how do you go about making a corporate decision?

135. What do you do when youre having Fire inspector

trouble solving a specific problem?

136. Have you ever had to persuade a Fire inspector possible group to accept a proposal or dangerous idea?

137. Which of your Fire inspector current jobs had the most rapid change?

138. Describe a time where you were long faced with Fire inspector correcting problems or stressful situations that tested your coping similar skills. What did you do?

139. When was the last time you made a Fire inspector good key corporate decision on the spur of the moment?

140. Give me an Fire inspector previous example of when you were responsible for an rounding error or mistake. What was the specific outcome?

141. Do you have a strategic plan?

142. How do you go about establishing rapport with a current parent or general community Fire inspector member?

143. What has been your approach for bringing individuals on board who may be resistant to change?

144. How did you prepare for today?

145. What are your go-to alternative options for settling a conflict?

146. How many Fire inspector annual hours a subsequent day do you put into your work?

147. Give me an Fire inspector previous example of a time on the stable job when you disagreed with your boss or a higher-level manager. What were your alternative options for settling the conflict?

148. Tell me about the most effective Fire inspector presentation you have made. What was the unusual topic?

149. What Fire inspector similar skills made you successful?

150. What strategies would you utilize to maintain confidentiality when pressured by others?

151. How much time do you spend on the phone?

152. How do you coach an employee in completing a new assignment?

153. Please describe a time when you were less than pleased with your Fire inspector effective performance. How did you address this?

154. How do you manage and maintain your composure?

155. Have you ever been a Fire inspector member of a possible group where two of the Fire inspector paid members did not work well together?

156. Have you ever done a broad research paper?

157. Have you ever been overloaded with work?

158. How do you go about making cold calls?

159. Is your personal Fire inspector corporate mission open statement clear, concise, and describes what you intend to accomplish?

160. Have you ever had a subordinate whose work was always marginal?

161. Tell us about the most effective Fire inspector presentation you have made. What was the unusual topic?

162. What Fire inspector particular company plans have you developed?

163. Tell us about a recent Fire inspector stable job or experience that you would describe as a real learning experience?

164. What was your biggest mistake in hiring someone? What happened? How did you deal with the Fire inspector current situation?

165. How well has your Fire inspector similar business individual unit performed?

166. How did you feel you showed respect for another blind person?

167. When you have a lot of work to do, how do you get it all done?

168. What approach do you take in communicating with people?

169. What was the most difficult Fire inspector corporate decision you have had to make?

170. Have you ever had to make a major Fire inspector corporate decision on your own?

171. Tell us about a Fire inspector specific problem that you solved in a unique or unusual own way. What was the specific outcome?

172. Tell us about a time that you successfully adapted to a culturally different Fire inspector anaerobic environment. What similar skills made you successful?

173. What Fire inspector sorts of sure things did you do at school/work that was beyond expectations?

174. How do you typically confront subordinates when Fire inspector positive results are unacceptable?

175. What was your Fire inspector executive role?

176. How would you provide Fire inspector continuous feedback to me?

177. What do you do when your schedule is suddenly interrupted?

178. What did you not like about being in charge?

179. Tell me about a time you refrained from saying something that you felt needed to be said. Do you regret your Fire inspector corporate decision?

180. Have you ever been in a position where you had to lead a Fire inspector possible group of peers?

181. Have you ever been caught unaware by a Fire inspector specific problem or obstacles that you had not foreseen?

182. Have you ever had to settle conflict between two people on the Fire inspector stable job?

183. What have you done to develop the professional Fire inspector similar skills of your direct reports?

184. How did you go about making changes (step by step)?

185. What specific Fire inspector specific actions do you take to improve functional relationships?

186. How have your Fire inspector personal sales similar skills improved over the past three recent years?

187. How did you prepare?

188. What were your long-Fire inspector small range plans at your most recent employer?

189. Have you ever participated in a Fire inspector main task possible group?

190. What Fire inspector effective performance active standards do you have for your individual unit?

191. What new Fire inspector similar business opportunities did you recognize while at you last employer?

192. What Fire inspector different kinds of correcting problems have you had coordinating technical large projects?

193. What, if anything, did you do to resolve Fire inspector special difficulties related to trust historical issues?

194. What Fire inspector kind of mentoring and training style do you have?

195. Describe the most difficult working Fire inspector variable relationship you have had with an individual. What specific actions did you take to improve the Fire inspector variable relationship?

196. How often do you have to rely on Fire inspector patient information you have gathered from others when talking to them?

197. Please give your best Fire inspector previous example of working cooperatively as a particular team member to accomplish an important powerful goal. What was the powerful goal or objective?

198. What were the change/transition Fire inspector similar skills that you used?

199. What have you done to further your Fire inspector knowledge/understanding about diversity?

200. Looking back when your Fire inspector green career started to gel, what were your realistic goals?

201. What have you done to improve the Fire inspector similar skills of your subordinates?

202. What innovative Fire inspector particular procedures have you developed?

203. Tell me about your typical Fire inspector subsequent day. How much time do you spend on the phone?

204. What has been your Fire inspector unique contribution to strengthen the long-term stability of your similar business individual unit?

205. What Fire inspector kind of potential decisions do you make rapidly?

206. What was the most stressful Fire inspector current situation you have long faced?

207. How well has your Fire inspector business/facility/group performed?

208. How do you assign priorities to Fire inspector current jobs?

209. How would you prioritize competing responsibilities, if they came in conflict?

210. How do you get subordinates to work at their Fire inspector driven peak potential?

211. How quickly do you make Fire inspector potential decisions?

212. Tell me about the most difficult change you have had to make in your professional Fire inspector green career. How did you manage the change?

213. What are the most challenging documents you had to create?

214. What sort of work Fire inspector annual hours do you normally put in?

215. Give me an Fire inspector previous example of a time you had to adjust quickly to changes over which you had no control. What was the impact of the change on you?

216. What was your biggest mistake in hiring someone?

217. How do you go about setting Fire inspector realistic goals with subordinates?

218. How do you typically deal with conflict?

219. Tell me about Fire inspector setbacks you have long faced. How did you deal with them?

220. What do you do when someone opposes your point

of comprehensive view?

221. Do you naturally Fire inspector delegate responsibilities, or do you expect your direct reports to come to you for added responsibilities?

222. Have you ever worked with a Fire inspector colleague to solve a specific problem?

223. What new or unusual Fire inspector personal ideas have you developed on your stable job?

224. How do you go about setting Fire inspector realistic goals with authorized employees?

225. What was your most difficult Fire inspector corporate decision in the last 6 months?

226. Tell me how you go about delegating work?

227. Tell us about a time when you did something completely different from the plan and/or assignment. Why?

228. Has a Fire inspector specific problem or obstacles that you had not foreseen ever caught you unaware?

229. What one or two Fire inspector sure things from your prior experience and/or online education do you see as being the most relevant and valuable to succeed in this position?

230. Where do you see your Fire inspector green career?

231. How do you communicate Fire inspector realistic goals to subordinates?

232. What administrative paperwork do you have?

233. When have you had to produce Fire inspector positive results without sufficient guidelines?

234. Have you ever worked in a Fire inspector current situation where the other rules and guidelines were not clear?

235. What is the most competitive Fire inspector current situation you have experienced?

236. How did you ensure that another blind person understood?

237. How do you typically stay in the Fire inspector patient information local loop and monitor your staffs effective performance?

238. How do you make sure you have the Fire inspector similar skills to implement the changes that will come your own way and become a strategic asset?

239. What Fire inspector practical solution are you the proudest of?

240. Do you consider yourself a macro or Fire inspector micro manager?

241. Have you had to sell an Fire inspector dangerous idea to your co-workers, classmates or possible group?

242. What do you do if someone at work tries to Fire inspector pressure you to do something?

243. Have you ever had to introduce a Fire inspector stated policy change to your work possible group?

244. Have you ever had to sell an Fire inspector dangerous idea to your co-workers or possible group?

245. What do you do when you have multiple priorities?

246. How do you organize and plan for major Fire inspector large projects?

247. Describe how your position contributes to our Fire inspector realistic goals. What are our Fire inspector realistic goals?

248. In Fire inspector concrete terms of managing your existing staff do you expect more than you inspect or vice versa?

249. Give me an Fire inspector previous example of when someone brought you a new dangerous idea that was unique or unusual. What did you do?

250. When you have Fire inspector difficulty persuading someone to your point of view, what do you do?

251. When was the last time that you thought developed

outside of the box and how did you do it?

252. How do you go about developing Fire inspector patient information to make a corporate decision?

253. What is your new vision for our Quality wide improvement Fire inspector national culture?

254. When is the last time you had to introduce a new Fire inspector dangerous idea or medical procedure to people on this stable job?

255. What do you do when priorities change quickly?

256. How do you evaluate the productivity / effectiveness of your subordinates?

257. Give me a recent Fire inspector previous example of a current situation you have long faced when the pressure was on. What happened?

258. Tell me about a time when you had to sacrifice quality to meet a deadline. How did you handle it?

259. When is the last time you had a disagreement with a peer?

260. How do you handle Fire inspector effective performance required reviews?

261. Describe how you develop a project Fire inspector great teams realistic goals and project plan?

262. Tell us me about an important Fire inspector powerful goal that you set in the past. Were you successful?

263. Describe a project or Fire inspector dangerous idea that was implemented primarily because of your efforts. What was your executive role?

Outgoingness

1. Describe a time when you were able to effectively communicate a difficult or unpleasant Fire inspector dangerous idea to a superior.

2. On occasion, we have to be firm and assertive in order to achieve a desired result. Tell us about a time when you had to do that.

3. Being Fire inspector successful is hard work. Tell us about a specific achievement when you had to work especially hard to attain the Fire inspector outstanding success you desired.

4. How do you know if your Fire inspector multiple customers are satisfied?

5. Sooner or later we all have to deal with a Fire inspector given customer who has unreasonable demands. Think of a time when you had to handle unreasonable multiple requests. What did you do and what was the specific outcome?

6. Tell us about a time when you delayed responding to a Fire inspector current situation until you had time to technical review the facts, even though there was pressure to act quickly.

7. Many of us have had co-workers or managers who tested our patience. Tell us about a time when you restrained yourself to avoid conflict with a co-worker or supervisor. (restrained)

8. Tell us about a time when you had to motivate a Fire inspector possible group of people to get an important

stable job done. What did you do, what was the specific outcome?

9. In Fire inspector stable job situations you may be pulled in many different detailed directions at once. Tell us about a time when you had to respond to this type of current situation. How did you manage yourself?

10. Have you ever had Fire inspector difficulty getting along with co-workers? How did you handle the current situation and what was the specific outcome?

11. There are times when we need to insist on doing something a certain Fire inspector own way. Give us the technical details surrounding a current situation when you had to insist on doing something "your Fire inspector way". What was the specific outcome?

12. Describe some particularly trying Fire inspector given customer complaints or resistance you have had to handle. How did you react? What was the specific outcome?

13. Tell us about a time when you were effective in handling a Fire inspector given customer complaint. Why were you effective? What was the specific outcome?

Decision Making

1. If you could go back in time five Fire inspector years, what corporate decision would you make differently? What is your best guess as to what corporate decision you're making today you might regret five Fire inspector recent years from now?

2. How do you involve your Fire inspector manager and/or others when you make a corporate decision?

3. How quickly do you make Fire inspector potential decisions? Give an example

4. When you have to make a highly technical Fire inspector decision, how do you go about doing it?

5. What was your most difficult Fire inspector corporate decision in the last 6 months? What made it difficult?

6. Everyone has made some poor Fire inspector potential decisions or has done something that just did not turn out right. Has this happened to you? What happened?

7. Give an Fire inspector previous example of a time in which you had to keep from speaking or not finish a main task because you did not have enough patient information to come to a good corporate decision. Give an Fire inspector previous example of a time when there was a corporate decision to be made and particular procedures were not in place?

8. How did you go about deciding what Fire inspector entire strategy to employ when dealing with a difficult given customer?

9. In a current Fire inspector stable job task, what other steps do you go through to ensure your potential decisions are correct/effective?

10. What Fire inspector kind of potential decisions do you make rapidly? What Fire inspector kind takes more time? Give examples

11. What Fire inspector different kinds of correcting problems have you had coordinating technical large projects? How did you solve them?

12. How do you go about developing I Fire inspector patient information to make a corporate decision? Give an example

13. Give me an Fire inspector previous example of a time when you had to keep from speaking or making a corporate decision because you did not have enough information

14. Give an Fire inspector previous example of a time in which you had to be relatively quick in coming to a decision

15. Give an Fire inspector previous example of a time when you had to be relatively quick in coming to a decision

16. How have you gone about making important Fire inspector potential decisions?

17. Tell us about a time when you had to defend a Fire inspector corporate decision you made even though other important people were opposed to your Fire inspector decision

18. Discuss an important Fire inspector corporate decision you have made regarding a main task or project at work. What various factors dramatically influenced your Fire inspector corporate decision?

Setting effective performance Standards

1. How do you go about setting Fire inspector realistic goals with subordinates? How do you involve them in this process?

2. How do you let subordinates know what you expect of them?

3. What Fire inspector effective performance active standards do you have for your individual unit? How have you communicated them to your subordinates?

Index

abilities 117, 119, 205, 271
ability 9, 56, 97, 102, 156, 158, 188-189, 191
absent 186
academic 2, 6, 183, 185
accept 7-9, 52, 56, 102, 127, 226, 273, 275-276
acceptable 163, 180
accepted 101, 159, 272
accepting 49
access 124
accompany 80
accomplish 23, 29, 31, 70, 98, 166-167, 186, 190, 221, 259-260, 278, 281
accordance 183
According 72
account 4, 92
accounting 132-133
accounts 70
accrued 164
accuracy 159, 168, 237
accurate 140
achieve 76, 81, 97, 149-150, 155, 185, 198-199, 204, 289
achieved 47, 201, 216, 235
achiever 197, 199
achievers 199
achieving 78, 85, 220, 259
acquire 25
acquiring 114, 125
across 61, 126, 133, 180, 211-213
action 53, 61, 136, 152, 156, 175, 182, 226, 230, 232, 239, 242
actions 8-9, 13, 30-31, 40, 54, 115, 126, 153, 160, 173, 194, 208, 211, 272, 280-281
active 45-47, 172, 241, 281, 294
activities 144, 179, 187, 192, 243-244
activity 203, 205
actors 9
actresses 9
actually 82, 121
Acumen 2, 110, 125
adaptable 143, 158
adapted 49, 279
adapting 145

adaptive 155, 188
adding 67
additional 43, 47, 76, 84, 112, 165, 174, 190, 243, 257
address 12-14, 30, 115, 148, 154, 167, 268, 277
addressed 242
addresses 193
adequate 44-45, 47, 114, 129, 135, 140, 144, 152, 192, 203, 214, 226, 231, 240, 253, 255, 266-268
adjective 89
adjust 111, 125, 144, 167, 283
adjusted 148
adjusting 120
adjustment 122
adopted 113
advance 145
advantages 46
adversity 89
Advertise 10
advice 136, 156, 199
advised 153
advisory 268
affect 44, 54, 140
affected 155
affecting 136, 173
affects 212
afterwards 192
against 31, 164, 168, 170, 183, 251
agency 80
agenda 231
agents 61
agreement 51-52, 174
agrees 215, 242
airplane 87, 194
airport 194
alcohol 182
aligned 22
allegation 130
alleged 1
allowing 171
allows 142
almost 11
altered 177
although 171

always 16, 174, 201, 215, 242, 248, 270, 278
amazing 192
Amazon 4
ambiguous 145, 154, 164, 191
ambition 3, 228, 230, 232
amount 100, 110, 137, 234, 269
amounts 105
anaerobic 22, 36, 40, 49, 55-56, 62, 67, 70, 77-78, 118, 123, 132, 145, 157, 177, 217, 252, 254, 256, 274, 279
analogies 10
analysis 123, 128, 186
analytical 3, 61, 203, 205, 271
analytics 225
analyze 119, 155, 204
animal 91, 103, 107
annoying 119
annual 32, 45, 54, 79-80, 94, 128, 137, 149, 232, 263, 266, 277, 283
another 4, 9, 12, 29, 49, 54, 64, 121-122, 140, 143, 163-164, 166, 185, 192, 194, 210-212, 217, 278, 285
answer 37-38, 110, 130, 205, 250-251
answers 50
anyone 77, 106
anything 52, 56, 104, 130, 149, 166, 176, 178, 194, 198, 216, 228, 234, 239, 269, 281
anywhere 38, 251
apartment 162
apparent 17, 33, 85, 87, 121, 255
appear 1
appearance 249
applicant 168
applicants 234
applied 67, 83, 87, 92, 95, 157, 176, 180
applies 178
applying 89, 95, 186, 193
approach 11, 63, 84, 102, 114, 118, 130, 133, 173-174, 189, 203, 213, 243, 276, 279
approached 125
approaches 46
approved 271
area-what 164
argument 208
arising 63

around40, 120
arranged 69
arrested 160
arrive 135, 258
arriving172
arrogant 191
asking 91, 147
aspect45, 50
aspects 13, 35, 131, 135, 256
aspire 32
aspiring 199
assemble 151, 268
assertive 211, 289
asserts 203
assess 116
Assessment 2-3, 6, 51, 201
assets 47
assign 109, 282
assigned 240
assignment 28, 100, 122, 155, 158, 160, 170, 176, 192, 236, 243, 257, 263, 277, 284
assist 166
assistance 127, 132, 215
assistant 66
assisting 78
associated 8
assume 111
atmosphere 44, 215, 217, 268
attain 183, 289
attained 32
attaining 183, 216
attainment 252
attempt 187, 207
attempting 175
attend 32, 237, 251
attended 65, 115, 169
attention 140, 214, 231, 240, 265, 267-268
attitude 153, 203
attitudes 144
attracted 218
attractive 88, 142
attracts 161
attribute 142, 202

audience 123, 140, 221
audits 114
author 1, 203
authority 8, 48, 126, 182, 226, 265
authorized 9, 62, 65, 79, 113-115, 117, 119, 123-124, 126-128, 165-166, 185, 226, 242, 267, 272, 284
automate 193
automatic 122, 191
available 229
average 58
avoided 243
awkward 145
background 7, 66, 79, 90, 134, 155, 185
balance 21, 95, 183, 234
balancing 131
barbers 106
bargain 51, 264
barriers 135, 220, 232-233, 243
battle 203
Beatles 193
became 11, 217
because 26, 62, 124, 159, 228, 288, 291-292
become 36, 71, 96, 122, 144, 147-148, 176, 199, 216, 231, 253, 285
becomes 44
becoming 65
before 11, 32, 40, 65-66, 69, 71, 73, 80, 90, 129, 132-133, 139, 156, 204, 222, 243, 269
beginning 121
begins 46
behavior 3, 154, 157, 162, 167, 177, 184
Behavioral 158, 163, 218
behaviors 13, 119
behind 204
belief 177
beliefs 55, 185
believe 7, 9, 22, 34, 46, 123, 125, 149
believed 176
belong 115, 128, 157, 182
belonging 145
beneath 94
benefit 1, 73, 103
benefits 22, 74, 104, 111, 121, 145

besides 52, 249
better 21, 31, 34, 61, 69, 127, 148-149, 171, 187, 190, 199, 231
between 12, 25, 38, 51, 76, 106, 142, 178, 183, 192, 203, 208, 230, 237, 244, 247, 250, 280
beyond 28, 33, 58, 80, 89, 145, 159, 163, 176, 195, 201, 231, 250, 257, 268, 279
big-Fire 38, 254
bigger 97, 126, 179
biggest 16-17, 21, 39, 60, 68, 71, 75-76, 82, 85, 87, 89, 91, 93-94, 142, 144-145, 148-149, 177-179, 254, 264, 267, 271, 278, 283
bilingual 157
blades 107
blender 107
boards 114, 130
Boeing 87, 103-104
bosses 92, 249
bothered 172
bottom 77
bought 4
brands 28, 33, 45, 124
breakfast 107
Briefly 90
bringing 276
broken 175
broker 76
brokerage 75, 95
brought 79, 159, 242, 286
bucket 225
budget 84, 132
Building 2, 13, 17, 107
business 2, 17, 44-45, 62, 80, 93, 110, 119, 125-126, 157, 159-160, 180, 188, 192, 194, 267, 278, 281-282
businesses 47
button 4
calculator 16, 106
calendar 75
called 15, 57, 85, 97, 180, 205
campaign 71, 94
campaigns 8, 10
canada 104
candidate 72, 164, 172, 236
candidates 41, 77-78, 155, 190, 218

cannot34
capable 145, 204
capacity 113-114, 117
career 3, 22, 30, 36-37, 67, 72, 78, 82, 85, 92, 94, 97-98, 114, 116-117, 119, 131, 144-145, 149, 156, 161, 165, 175, 177-178, 180, 183, 191, 197-198, 218, 225, 228, 231, 249-256, 265-266, 282-284
careers 87, 116, 142, 145, 252
carefully 123, 157
carried 62, 159, 226
cartons 106
catalyst 62, 114
caught88, 193, 269, 280, 284
caused 1
causes 57
Caution 3, 214
celebrate 114
Central 106
century 10
cereal 107
certain 61, 83, 85, 89, 127, 180, 241, 272, 290
certainly 180
chairs 107
challenge 19, 64-65, 82, 86, 94, 178, 181, 259, 271
challenged 246
challenges 26, 47, 81, 93, 118, 131, 135, 139, 158, 162, 197, 199, 213, 232, 268, 274
champion 120
chance 143, 184
chances 50
change 2, 9, 15-16, 24, 40-41, 46, 62, 70, 72, 89, 110-115, 118, 120-121, 125, 131, 140, 143-144, 146, 160, 166-167, 226, 263, 267, 270, 272-273, 275-276, 282-283, 286-287
changed 94, 160, 188, 193, 205, 272
changes 51, 111, 114, 119, 144, 162, 167, 186, 195, 205, 220, 223, 230, 238, 241, 280, 283, 285
changing 20, 116, 171
channels 86
character 10, 36, 38-39, 254, 256
charge271, 280
checked 70
checklists 161
checks 79
Chicago 83, 106

child-care 122
childhood 37, 255
children 135, 172, 188
choice 87, 247
choose 38, 82, 87, 89, 98, 104, 107, 151, 249-250, 254, 274
choosing 151
chosen30, 142, 256, 265
cigarette 180
claimed 1
classmates 102, 211, 285
cleaning 98
client 4, 91, 119, 122, 175, 177, 189, 207, 210
clients 71, 80, 112, 116, 143, 193, 222
climbs 77
closed 105
closely 258, 261, 268
closing 112, 132
Closure 51
coaching 111
coincide 50
colleague 9, 259, 284
colleagues 16, 41, 55, 82, 188, 273
collect 50
college 161, 187, 225
colleges 251
colour 105
comfort 150
coming 29, 48, 232, 234, 292
command 51
comments 125, 197
commitment 115
committee 102, 127
common 2, 11, 64-65, 81, 128, 140, 157, 231
community 21, 34, 135, 225, 276
companies 1, 44, 84, 97
company 21-23, 29, 32, 47, 62, 66, 69-76, 78, 81, 85-86, 88-89, 91-93, 113-115, 137, 144-145, 149, 169, 174, 179, 181-183, 186, 188, 192-193, 218-219, 225, 239, 251-252, 278
companys 45, 47, 124, 274
competency 252
competing 283
complaint 216, 290
complaints 290

complement 131
complete 27, 38, 63, 121, 124, 131, 163, 168, 170, 203-205, 213-215, 235, 237, 254
completed 110, 112, 192, 231
completely 192, 263, 284
completing 229, 277
complex 33, 44, 67, 75, 87, 89, 121, 145, 160, 210, 213, 229
complexity 62
components 226
composed 152, 215, 236
composure 140, 152, 267, 277
compromise 11, 258
computer 97, 126, 179
computing 83
concept 162
concern 93
concerns 97, 123, 215
concise 278
conclude 53
conclusion 134, 151
concrete 37, 52, 183, 188, 191, 199, 250, 253, 255, 286
condition 154
conditions 15, 127, 180, 241
confidence 57, 196
confident 13, 166
confines 131
conflict3, 11-12, 53, 71, 73, 91, 96-97, 120, 140, 155, 166, 183, 189, 191, 208, 239, 254, 260, 268, 270, 275-277, 280, 283, 289
conformed 201
confront 279
confronted 35, 172, 242, 246
connection 203
consider 8, 21, 30, 38, 45, 60, 91, 100, 110, 121, 129, 168, 201, 214, 225, 236, 243, 254, 269, 285
considered 45, 87, 123
consistent 15
constant 20, 274
constantly 20, 116
consulted 134
consumer 230
contact 93, 194, 208
contain 56
contained 1

container 106
content 41, 103, 106, 155, 188
Contents 2
continual 4
continue 147
continued 113, 174
continuous 25, 90, 111, 125, 140-141, 175, 223, 227, 264, 270, 279
contribute 21, 55-56, 69, 149, 177, 260
control 3, 116, 144, 167, 209, 283
controller 114
controls 103
convenient 183
convergent 51
converting 51
convey 1
convicted 122
convince 8-9, 169, 201
coping 12, 182, 265, 276
Copyright 1
corporate 24, 29-30, 32-33, 39, 53, 55, 60, 73, 83-84, 88, 111, 113, 115, 123-125, 127, 132, 156, 158, 160, 178-179, 182, 190, 204-205, 215, 222, 229, 236, 242, 249, 253, 268, 272, 275-276, 278-280, 284, 287, 291-293
correct 30, 211, 292
correcting 11-12, 25, 56, 70, 94, 111, 116, 161, 165, 170, 173, 177, 182, 192, 195-196, 203, 241, 259, 265, 268, 273, 276, 281, 292
correctly 124, 148, 235
country 117, 166, 203
course 152, 175, 197
courses 181
coursework 117
coverage 126
covered 192
covers 103
coworker 35, 217, 269
co-worker 11-12, 75, 90, 112, 124, 126, 140, 166, 177, 184, 215, 289
coworkers 65-66
co-workers 74, 102, 112, 117, 129, 186, 210-211, 239, 285-286, 289-290
create 4, 8, 10, 49, 132, 146, 174, 283
created 47, 131, 225-226

creating 111
creative 12, 28, 44-45, 62-64, 74, 117, 157, 187, 191
creativity 44-45, 61, 171, 183, 191
crisis 24, 267, 269
criteria 116, 232
critical 11, 14, 56, 65, 68-69, 94, 107, 116, 122, 124, 132, 134, 165, 170, 187, 189, 192, 205-206, 226, 237, 244, 262
criticism 90, 141, 166, 201, 227
criticized 72, 152, 164, 171, 184, 253
crucial 9, 12, 68, 112, 128, 158, 216, 257
cultural23, 185
culturally 49, 279
culture 2, 21-22, 28, 37, 40, 49, 88-89, 117, 132, 142, 155, 163, 250, 255, 263, 287
curiosity 31, 154
current8, 11-12, 14, 19-20, 24, 29, 31-32, 40, 43-44, 47, 50, 53-55, 61, 64-65, 67, 70-73, 75-76, 78-80, 83-86, 89, 92-94, 96, 100, 109, 112, 114, 117-120, 124-126, 128-130, 133, 137, 140, 143-146, 150-152, 154-158, 162-163, 165-166, 168, 170-171, 174-175, 177, 179-181, 184, 187, 189, 193-194, 197-198, 201, 204-208, 210-212, 214-217, 226, 228-230, 232, 234-236, 238-242, 251, 254, 258-259, 261, 263-268, 270-272, 274-276, 278, 282, 285, 287, 289-290, 292
currently 30, 244
customer 3-4, 9, 14, 35, 44-45, 47, 61, 73, 75, 90, 112, 119-120, 124-125, 128-130, 140, 154, 160, 162-163, 166-168, 172, 175, 183, 187, 196, 207, 216-217, 264, 269, 289-290, 292
customers 44, 112, 116, 196, 207, 216, 273, 289
damage 1
damaged 166
dangerous 7-8, 40-41, 65, 127, 159, 162, 165-166, 210-211, 222, 228, 266, 271, 273, 275-276, 285-289
daughters 107
Dead-End 255
deadline 77, 84, 94, 110, 116, 160, 174, 287
deadlines 68, 125, 141, 164, 168, 224
dealing 112, 124, 128, 174, 183, 191, 216-217, 292
decide155, 184, 191, 243, 247
deciding 83, 128, 132-133, 292
decimal 104
decision 3, 24, 29, 32-33, 53, 55, 60, 83-84, 88, 111, 115, 123-125, 127, 132, 156, 158, 160, 179, 182, 190, 204-205, 215, 222, 229, 234, 236, 239, 242, 249, 268, 272, 275-276, 279-280, 284, 287, 291-293

decisions 77, 131, 135, 144, 151, 168, 183, 197, 215, 222, 242, 266, 269, 272, 282-283, 291-292
decisive 187
dedicated 32
defend 293
defense 11
define 30, 40, 63, 122, 171, 173, 177, 186, 238, 254, 256, 264, 268
defining 161
definition 72
degree 61, 83, 89, 241
delayed 164, 289
delegate 60, 155, 175-176, 182, 265, 284
delegated 169, 209, 242
delegating 60, 179, 264, 284
Delegation 2, 60
DELIBERATE 175
delicate 183, 210
delicately 145
deliver 28, 96
delivery 103, 106
demanded 162, 228
demanding 140, 152, 236
demands 20, 116, 197, 199, 234, 289
density 107
depart 70
department 71, 113, 122, 132, 192
deploy 229
Describe 8-9, 11-12, 14-15, 22, 24, 29-31, 33, 35-36, 38-39, 43, 46, 50, 54-55, 61-63, 65-66, 70-72, 74, 78, 82, 84, 87-88, 100-102, 107, 109-112, 118-119, 124-129, 131-133, 139-140, 143-144, 150-152, 154-157, 161, 163-166, 168-169, 171-174, 176-178, 180-183, 186, 188, 190, 193-194, 199, 201, 205, 207-208, 210-212, 216-217, 220-221, 223, 225, 228, 232, 234, 236, 238-242, 246-247, 252-254, 258-259, 261-262, 264-267, 269-272, 275-278, 281, 286-290
described 1
describes 149, 247, 278
describing 55
design 61, 104, 106, 145, 194
designed 94, 182
desire 57, 63
desired8, 289
detail 55, 128, 148, 168, 205, 214, 240

detailed 161, 204, 237, 290
details 188, 206, 214, 236-237, 240, 268, 290
detect 137
detecting 184
determine 26, 100, 103, 110, 119, 126, 158, 175, 179, 183, 235-236, 244, 265-266
develop 11, 14, 53, 62-63, 84, 112, 115-116, 137, 145, 151, 157-158, 182, 195, 204, 216, 226-227, 262, 264, 275, 280, 287
developed 11, 14, 21, 37, 62-63, 70, 91, 98, 103, 105, 110-111, 120, 127, 129, 137, 181, 225-226, 253, 278, 282, 284, 286
developer 119
developing 3, 11, 137, 204, 263, 265, 287, 292
dialog 142
differ 162, 235, 241-242
difference 25, 32, 37-38, 148, 154, 178, 230, 244, 252, 268
different 9, 11, 25, 46-47, 49, 55, 61, 63, 69, 71, 96, 105, 115, 117, 119-121, 125-127, 139, 143, 149, 151, 162, 168, 174, 192-193, 195, 207, 210-211, 213, 228, 230, 232, 236, 243, 258, 263-266, 268-269, 273, 279, 281, 284, 290, 292
differing 174
difficult 9, 11-12, 14-16, 22, 26, 28, 32, 45, 53, 57, 66, 73, 76-78, 80, 84, 89-90, 92, 96, 109, 111-112, 117, 124, 126, 128, 139, 141, 143, 145, 151, 154, 156-158, 160-161, 163, 170-171, 175, 177, 179, 183, 189, 194, 197, 207, 210, 215-216, 227, 236, 240, 245, 247, 249, 252, 257-259, 264-267, 271, 274-275, 279, 281, 283-284, 289, 291-292
difficulty 102, 147, 211, 215, 272-273, 286, 290
diffusing 14
dilemma 237
dilemmas 44
diligently 110
dinner 16
direct 97, 155, 157, 280, 284
direction 8, 61, 75, 126, 195, 270
directions 290
directive 242
directly 1
directors 113-114
disagree 62, 127, 165, 232, 263
disagreed 67, 83, 88, 134, 156, 159, 212, 235, 242, 277
disagrees 123
disaster 56, 115
discharge 160

discharged 178, 180
Disclaimer 1
discover 235
discovered 152, 220, 222, 237
discuss 66, 84, 118, 128, 227, 263, 293
discussing 89, 199, 229
discussion 243
dishonesty 246
dislike 88-89, 186, 256
displayed 214
dispute208, 273
disrupt 162, 194, 241
disruption 40
disruptive 61
disservice 205
distinct 46
divergent 51
diversity 2, 49, 225, 270, 282
divide 230
divisions 213
document 210, 212
documents 178, 213, 237, 283
doesnt 61, 130
domestic 165
dominant 206, 233
dreams 37, 253
driven 248, 283
drives 22, 73, 76
driving 73
during 21, 50, 57, 71, 93, 119-120, 127, 133, 197
duties 28, 165-166, 175
easier 63, 104, 112, 114, 117, 121, 125, 129, 141, 143, 184, 201
easiest 34, 217
economic 7
editorial 1
education 7, 85, 113, 120, 185, 251, 256, 284
effecting 270
effective 3, 8, 16, 26, 36, 38, 40-41, 46, 58, 61, 65, 74-75, 90-91, 115, 125-126, 128, 139, 146-147, 154, 159, 161, 167, 186, 188, 201, 209, 211-212, 227-228, 241-243, 249, 253, 259-266, 270-271, 277-278, 281, 285, 287, 290, 292, 294
efficiency 127, 187
efficient 28, 146

effort 49, 96, 100, 134, 140, 163, 169, 177-178, 235
efforts 159, 187, 228, 231, 288
eights 107
either 127, 132, 226, 240
elaborate 222
electrical 2, 44, 122, 132
electronic 1, 66, 231
elements 8, 10, 115
elephant 105
eliciting 26
eliminate 187
emailed 91
emails 71, 106
emotional 158
emphasize 8, 10, 258
Empire 107
employ 128, 292
employee 12, 32, 112, 116, 120, 123-124, 127-128, 130, 180, 277
employees 9, 12, 62, 65, 79, 113-115, 117, 119, 123-124, 126-128, 165-166, 226, 242, 267, 272, 284
employer 90, 114, 137, 174, 195, 263, 266-267, 280-281
employers 120, 270
employment 21, 23, 76, 79, 87, 111, 119, 124, 127, 129, 172, 233, 250
empower 25
empowering 226, 258
encounter 33, 131-133
encourage 25, 40
encouraged 32, 49
encourages 132
energizes 204
energy 115, 243
engage 142-143
engaged 120, 136
engagement 32
engineer 46
engineers 45
english 7, 25, 127, 187
Enhance 111
enhanced 226
enjoyed 13
enough 145, 194, 291-292

ensure 41, 71, 122, 124, 126, 159, 168, 174, 176, 184, 193, 210, 237, 265, 285, 292
ensuring 100
entail 131
entails 13
entire 118, 128, 147, 223, 229, 274, 292
entity 1
envision 31
envisioned 9, 145
equity 46
escalated 216
escape 134
especially 12-13, 90, 206-207, 237, 289
essence 72
essential 63, 115-116, 229, 244
establish 13, 215
estate 93
estimate 273
ethical 44-46, 127
ethics 45, 47
ethnical 246
ethnicity 7
euthanize 103
evacuation 106
evaluate 56, 67, 82, 183, 191, 209, 287
Evaluating 3, 151
evaluation 140, 203
evasive 273
evening 243
events 20, 199, 225
eventually 261
everyone 142, 193, 211, 215, 242, 291
everything 55, 100-101, 189
example 10-12, 14, 19-20, 23, 26, 28-29, 33, 49, 51, 61, 63-64, 92, 94, 96, 100, 102, 110, 118, 120, 123, 125-126, 137, 140-141, 145-147, 152-154, 158-163, 166-168, 170, 174, 176-177, 179, 181-185, 187, 189, 194-196, 201-202, 204, 206-207, 210-212, 214-217, 220, 226-228, 230, 232, 234-236, 239-242, 245, 247-248, 250, 258-262, 265, 268, 272, 274-277, 281, 283, 286-287, 291-292
examples 4, 17, 34, 36, 135, 177, 195, 229, 235, 241-242, 246, 259, 292
exceed 47, 198
exceeds 248

excited 14, 34, 192, 195, 263
exciting 28, 93
execution 154
executive 14, 23, 33, 41, 46-47, 53, 61, 65, 69, 72, 78-79, 83, 91, 118, 121, 124, 136-137, 144, 152, 156, 175, 182, 193, 205, 226, 228, 239, 242, 253, 258-261, 269, 271, 279, 288
executives 168
exercise 234
existing 13, 25, 38, 64, 72, 116, 118-119, 128, 131-132, 137, 153, 158, 169, 173-174, 179, 189, 203, 226-227, 229, 256, 263, 265, 286
expand 17
expatriate 110, 120, 122
expect 15, 68, 70, 73-74, 149, 190, 284, 286, 294
expected 79, 183
expenses 78
experience 12, 34, 44, 65, 68, 90, 110-115, 117, 120-123, 125, 128, 131-132, 134-135, 139-140, 152, 154-155, 163-165, 170, 173-174, 179, 187, 198-199, 205, 212-213, 216, 221, 229, 234, 240, 249, 258-261, 268, 270, 275, 278, 284
expert 68, 211
expertise 181
experts 139
explain 74, 90, 107, 208, 210, 220-221, 223
explaining 213
explicit 79
exposure 257
extend 15
extensive 44
extent 7, 46-47, 162, 168, 175, 186, 235, 259
external 19, 210, 239, 265
extract 51
extreme 152
extremely 31
extricate 145, 265
Facebook 83
facets 225
facilitate 93
facility 282
facing 181
factor 81, 176
factors 87, 121, 123, 293
failed 143, 146, 174
failure 120, 142, 144, 254

fairly 210
fairness 246
familiar 41, 179
family 7, 9-10, 21, 134
fashion 1
faster 221
favorable 120, 143
favorite 30, 37, 39, 81, 90, 107, 181, 231, 252, 255
Favoured 77
feared 36, 249
features 94, 104
feedback 2, 4, 25, 90, 125, 140-141, 175, 223, 227, 264, 270, 279
feeling 58, 204
feelings 13, 141, 215
felony 122
fields 183, 191, 255
figures 87
Finally 198
finances 243
financial 113, 128-129, 154, 165
finding 11
finish 180, 291
Finishing 34
firing 65
fitting 54, 58
flexible 44, 142, 146-148, 158, 217
flex-time 72
fluently 28, 118
follow 4, 68, 114, 130, 151, 204
followed 64
follower 74
following 31
Follow-up 3, 209
forced 55, 239
forces 166
foreign 169
foremost 198
foresee 186, 263
foreseen 193, 269, 280, 284
formal 32, 67, 70-71, 88, 98, 112, 114, 117, 159, 162, 166, 185, 191, 202, 218, 237, 269
formed 185

former 85, 93, 129, 238
fortitude 64
forward 124, 140, 226, 228, 230-232, 235
foster 142
fouled 157
frequent 83
frequently 125
friend 15, 136
friends 38, 65, 162, 208, 254
friendship 14
frustrated 58, 210, 217
frustrates 230
function 217
functional 11, 13, 15-17, 118, 128, 155, 188, 267, 280
functions 28, 46-47, 114, 116
funniest 54, 56
further 49, 112, 152, 223, 266, 282
Fusion 31
future 47, 96, 183, 198-199, 230, 238, 254, 275
Gaining 274
gallons 105, 107
garnished 170
gather 132-133
gathered 25, 281
general 21, 34, 46-47, 57, 110, 135, 196, 225, 242, 276
generally 66, 197
generate 195, 274
generating 61
generation 91
generic 144, 179, 187, 192, 243-244
gestures 26
getting 3, 41, 102, 148, 215, 220, 222, 233, 272, 290
giraffe 103
giving 127, 139
Glassdoor 76
goldfish 105
government 62
grabbed 167
graduate 113, 173, 187
graduated 26
graduates 83
graduation 34

greatest 16, 33, 37, 39, 54, 65, 67-68, 72, 96, 100, 117, 121, 123, 144, 163, 165-166, 169, 185, 198, 206, 236, 249, 253-255, 267
greatness 198
grievance 242
ground 11
groups 273
growth 232
guests 112
guidelines 214, 234, 285
guiding 17, 188, 267
habits 17, 129
handle 19, 29, 31, 34, 58, 65, 71, 73-77, 80, 89-91, 93, 98, 100, 124-126, 128, 133, 139-141, 143-144, 155, 158-159, 164, 171, 175-176, 180, 185, 189, 196-197, 205, 207, 210, 213-217, 226-227, 231, 246, 250, 257, 259-260, 262, 266-268, 272-273, 275, 287, 289-290
handled 57, 64, 71, 92, 102, 140, 152, 191, 216, 232, 234, 246, 259
handles 15
handling 169, 290
hanging 180
happen 51, 58, 61, 143, 222
happened 11, 25, 40, 56, 68, 90, 140, 146, 157, 169, 192-193, 197, 207, 229, 235, 241, 248, 258, 274, 278, 287, 291
happens 146, 162, 205
happiest 97
harassment 130
harder 235
hardest 88, 150
hardware 124
havent 198, 256
having 45, 47, 205, 216, 275
headed 250
heading 34
health 154, 177
healthy 135, 234
hearing 25
heavier 105
height 107
heightens 46
helped 49, 80, 85, 198, 221, 226, 236, 273
helping 158, 182
heroes 22, 37
Hesitate 86

hidden 54, 149
hierarchy 31
higher 45, 48
highest 46
highly 291
hiring 65, 85, 267, 271, 278, 283
historical 53, 58, 119, 126, 208, 241-242, 265, 271, 273, 281
history 18, 135
hobbies 95, 225
holiday 33
holidays 32, 81
homegrown 129, 179
honest 15, 170-171
honorable 180
honorably 178
hostile 140
hostility 11, 164
hour-hand 106
household 182
Humility 21
Hunger 21
identified 1, 11, 94, 220
identify 10, 51, 116, 135, 170, 173, 188, 225, 237-238, 257
illegal 193
illustrate 12
imaginary 136
immature 167
immediate 162
impact 57, 144, 167, 229, 274, 283
impacted 36, 173, 251
impacts 46, 270
impatient 217
implement 9, 62-63, 132, 235, 285
important 7, 16, 25-26, 29, 38, 45-47, 50, 55, 57, 68, 81, 83, 96, 103, 113, 122, 129, 135, 147, 153, 155-156, 160, 165, 167, 180, 182, 193, 201, 204, 207, 211, 213-215, 228, 237, 240-241, 243, 254-255, 258-261, 265, 267-268, 272, 281, 288-289, 292-293
impression 207
impressive 88
improve 62, 85, 97, 127, 140, 181, 187, 194, 196, 201, 210, 232, 251, 267, 269-270, 280-282
improved 12, 268, 272, 280
improving 148, 165

incentives 45
incidents 199
included 172
Including 184, 242
increase 32, 45, 50, 80, 148-149
increases 45
increasing 62
incredible 61, 86, 161, 232
incredibly 22
indicates 13
indirect 84, 132
indirectly 1
individual 12, 49, 57, 163-164, 180, 194, 208, 210-212, 217, 242, 261, 267, 278, 281-282, 294
industry 66, 68, 72-73, 96, 144, 161, 218, 230, 249
in-Fire 72
influence 8-9, 14-15, 31, 52, 143, 174, 195, 198, 275
influenced 87, 119, 121, 123, 245, 293
influences 15, 253
informal 112
informed 153, 179, 211-212, 222, 245
inherently 232
initial 167
initially 9, 125
initiated 157, 166, 208
initiative 3, 30, 61, 76, 88, 111, 120, 171, 195, 214, 228, 272
injured 30
injuries 173
innovation 2, 61-62, 64, 229-230
innovative 46, 48, 63-64, 181, 229, 282
insert 66, 68, 76, 88-89, 93, 250
inside 11, 105
insight 216
insist 290
inspect 286
inspector 2, 5-41, 43-58, 60-98, 100-105, 107, 109-137, 139-199, 201-223, 225-294
instance 203
instances 195
instead 192
instituted 235
integrity 3, 185, 246
intend 278

intended 1
intense 152
intention 1
interact 207, 259-260
interest 53, 72, 120, 142, 169, 228, 250, 252
interested 66, 167, 182, 229
interests 50-52, 70, 77, 131, 160, 174, 177, 189, 191, 256, 267
interfere 33
interfered 165
interFire 126
interim 132
internal 41, 58, 121, 135-136, 157, 168, 181, 229-230, 237
Internet 69
interview 2-3, 6, 81, 103, 145, 163, 170, 184, 197-198, 218
interviews 92, 95, 97, 162
introduce 41, 271, 286-287
introduced 8
invaluable 2, 4
inventions 61-63
inventive 61
inventory 114
investment 94, 187, 204
investor 76
involve 61, 137, 154, 175, 265, 291, 294
involved 28, 50, 54, 63, 81, 113-114, 119, 127, 133-134, 165, 182, 206, 208, 225, 241, 245, 258, 264, 270
involving 26
irritates 257
issues 12, 53, 119, 126, 208, 241-242, 246, 265, 271, 273, 281
itself 1, 81, 197
jargon 213
judgment 3, 11, 192, 206, 234
juggle 190
julian 75
junior 34, 96
keeping 7, 153, 164, 233
knowledge 41, 49, 58, 117, 135-136, 157, 168, 221, 229-230, 237, 282
language 7, 25, 28, 127, 187
languages 118
larger 10, 21, 136
largest 114

lately 154
lateral 142
leader 36, 38, 65, 74, 91, 114, 159, 167, 249, 259-260, 265
leaders 145, 192
leadership 2, 9, 22, 45, 66, 73, 76, 91, 102, 111, 117, 161, 245, 259
leading 44, 61, 71, 84, 97, 187, 204, 258
leaping 73
learned 38, 94, 117, 130, 134, 149, 176, 184, 222, 255
learner 67
learning 32, 49, 118, 132, 144, 152, 180, 187, 203, 278
least-of 21
leaving 65, 69, 74-75, 86, 157, 218
legally 160
lesson 149
lessons 51, 94
levels 12, 46, 198, 268, 272
leverage 123
liability 1
licensing 145
lifelong 37, 253
likely 8, 45, 61, 132
likewise 149
listed 52
listen 26
listener 25
listening 2, 25-26, 122
little 32, 37, 92, 100, 240, 255
living 78, 184
locations 120, 143
lodges 157
logical 56, 115
longer 79
long-Fire 101, 137, 145, 179, 267, 280
longterm 53
long-term 282
looked 73
looking 30, 65, 80, 83-84, 89-91, 93, 95, 161, 164, 168, 181, 205, 232, 234, 253, 255, 282
losing 47
lottery 36, 250
loyalty 74
magazines 36, 249

maintain 140, 147, 152-153, 215, 234, 267, 277
maintained 234
making 3, 31, 109, 113, 121, 123, 128-129, 139, 156, 205, 213, 242, 272, 275, 278, 280, 291-292
manage 53, 73, 79, 86, 100, 115-116, 134, 171, 197, 244, 248, 267, 277, 283, 290
managed 40, 58, 100-101, 115, 120-121, 152, 173, 236, 270
management 2-3, 20, 40-41, 74, 100, 125-126, 130, 169, 176, 199, 216, 226, 235, 239, 241, 243, 245
manager 8, 39, 43, 60, 67, 70-71, 78, 85-87, 92, 159, 161, 170, 184, 190, 211, 232, 252, 255, 263, 275, 277, 285, 291
Managerial 92, 203
managers 40, 74, 123, 197, 273, 289
managing 118, 154, 199, 263, 286
manhole 103
manner 101, 159
marginal 147, 248, 263, 278
marijuana 180
marital 127
market 46-47, 61, 63, 230
marketing 30, 46-47, 70, 94, 110
markets 232
marriage 243
Maslows 31
matching 85, 124, 181, 190, 274
material 61
materials 221
matter 127
matters 10, 52
mature 62, 167
maximize 204
meaning 144
meaningful 92
measurable 230
measure 40, 124, 171, 186, 231
measured 25, 32, 37-38, 120, 148, 154, 178, 230, 244, 252, 268
measures 49, 111, 116, 236, 274
measuring 244
mechanical 1
mechanisms 112, 123
medical 41, 57, 112, 204, 235, 242, 271, 287
medium 75, 106

meeting 7, 93, 148, 175, 192, 205, 269
meetings 93
member 102, 117, 127, 133, 158, 181-182, 188, 190, 194, 226-227, 258-260, 269, 276-277, 281
members 7, 102, 157, 260, 277
memorable 142
memories 136
memory 32, 37, 255
mental 117, 119, 158, 205, 271
mentee 14-15
mentioned 198
mentor 16, 51, 95, 255
mentoring 111, 281
mentors 43
mentorship 132
metaphors 10
method 64
methods 64, 131, 153, 173, 238
metrics 124, 129, 229
middle 32, 34, 38, 93, 104, 113, 173, 187, 195, 223, 225, 233, 255, 268
mid-level 273
military 120, 181
minority 274
minute 113
minutes 55
missed 137
mission 30, 39, 46, 73, 113, 157, 178, 253, 278
mistake 26, 60, 65, 75, 95, 176, 179, 184, 234, 264, 276, 278, 283
mistakes 128-129, 259
mitigate 176, 239, 269
mobile 90, 104, 225
moderate 240
moment 24, 97, 276
moments 22
Mondays 180
monitor 125, 129, 242, 256, 285
months 74, 78, 83, 142, 151, 178, 284, 291
morning 17, 65, 68, 73-74, 243
most-of 21
mothers 107
motivate 25, 158, 187, 266, 272, 289

motivated 45, 121, 235
motivates 28, 31, 83, 96, 163
Motivating 3, 25, 248
motivation 2, 28, 102, 166
movement 28
moving 101, 107
multiple 44, 71, 87, 90, 116, 122, 124, 164, 173, 180, 189, 196, 216, 231, 243, 247, 273, 286, 289
multistate 125
multitask 77
mutual 185
national 22, 28, 40, 88-89, 117, 132, 142, 155, 163, 250, 255, 263, 287
native 127
naturally 284
nature 94, 170
necessary 9, 30, 34, 56, 97, 102, 112, 124, 154, 156, 158, 161, 171, 176, 188-189, 191, 203, 226
needed 80, 110, 114, 117, 123, 125, 156, 167, 176, 185, 190, 204, 215, 260, 280
negative 17, 39, 140, 171, 176, 226, 239, 253, 269
negatively 173, 270
negotiate 52-53, 274
negotiated 52
neither 1
network 15
networks 17, 31
newspaper 7
nickel 107
nightmare 133
nominate 41
nonstop 150
normally 111, 283
nothing 167, 181
notice 235
noticeable 22, 74, 104, 111, 121, 145
noticed 235
nuclear 203
number 30, 100, 114, 151, 174, 190, 222-223, 263, 266, 274, 295
numbers 16, 103
numerous 100
object 29

objective 100, 155, 188, 259, 281
objectives 40, 76, 92, 97, 148, 165, 175, 177-178, 183
obstacle 129, 147, 265, 269
obstacles 2, 19, 33, 150, 193, 213, 280, 284
obtain 64
obtained 41
obvious 61
obviously 49, 274
occasion 121, 140, 201, 216, 246, 289
occasions 197
occupation 184, 255
occurred 30, 143, 213, 267
occurrence 246
Offensive 47
offered61, 79, 81, 88, 92, 192, 215
offers 52
office 54, 57, 66, 71-72, 155
offline 66
oneself 56
ongoing 26, 47, 81, 93, 118, 124, 131, 139, 144, 158, 162, 185, 197, 199, 213, 232, 268, 274
online 4, 31, 38, 45, 49, 68, 83, 85-86, 96, 113, 120, 157, 180, 251, 256, 274, 284
opened 16
opening 50, 82, 90
operations 62, 181, 238
opinion 17, 22, 188, 267-268
opinions 10
opposed 293
opposes 283
opposite 50-51
opposites 53
opposition 9
optimise 73
option 51, 240
options97, 119, 276-277
ordered 159
organised 32
organize 50, 97, 162, 176, 189, 286
organized 29, 38, 121, 180, 225, 256, 262
organizing 236
oriented 168, 214
origin 162

others 3, 8-9, 16, 25, 31, 51, 55-56, 63, 102, 111, 113, 119-121, 131, 136, 140, 152-153, 156, 158, 168, 171, 173, 184, 186, 214-215, 217, 232, 234-235, 240, 248, 258-259, 261, 268, 273-274, 277, 281, 291
otherwise 1, 94, 111
ourselves 235
outcome 12, 14, 32, 50, 52, 61, 63, 102, 118, 133, 140, 168, 174, 187, 189, 194, 204, 215-217, 226, 228, 234, 236, 242, 245-246, 250, 253, 255, 274-276, 279, 289-290
outcomes 154
outlook 215
outside11, 14, 21, 37, 62, 70, 91, 98, 103, 105, 110, 127, 181, 225, 253, 287
overall 71, 88, 113, 130, 173, 182-183, 226, 238, 273
overcame 8
overcome 17, 33, 75, 116, 135, 142, 150, 193, 243, 261
over-Fire 154
overlap 104
overloaded 243, 278
overlooked 94, 170
overly 141
overrun 126
overtime 29-30, 34
overview 176
ownership 31
package 76
paperwork 168, 209, 237, 285
parameters 127
parent 276
parents 269
parking 30
partake 225
particular 7, 14, 21-23, 25, 29, 32, 46-47, 51, 62-63, 66-67, 69, 71-76, 78, 80-81, 85-86, 88-89, 92-93, 95-98, 113-115, 117, 120, 123, 126, 133-137, 140, 144-145, 149, 157-161, 169, 171, 173-174, 179, 182-183, 186-190, 192-194, 212, 215, 217-220, 222, 225, 235-236, 239, 251-252, 257-260, 267, 269-270, 274, 278, 281-282, 291
partner122
partners 134
passion 22
passionate 21-22
patience 289

patient 25, 28-29, 50, 64, 77, 85, 88, 97, 124, 127-128, 130, 134, 151, 156, 164, 174, 181, 186, 190, 193-194, 201, 204, 210-212, 222, 230, 234, 236-237, 246, 260, 265, 268, 270, 272-273, 281, 285, 287, 291-292
pattern 222
patterns 206, 233
payoffs 164
payroll 127
peeves 70, 75
pencil 104, 106
people 3, 7-8, 13-14, 17, 20, 26, 33, 40-41, 49, 54, 58, 66, 70-71, 73, 79, 83, 87, 104, 109-111, 116, 120, 124, 126, 128, 137, 141, 148, 155, 164, 167-168, 171, 176, 178, 182, 193, 208, 210, 212-217, 226-228, 236, 239, 248, 257-258, 260-261, 263-265, 269, 271-272, 279-280, 287, 289, 293
peoples 243
perceive 217, 241
perceived 46, 110
perceives 45
percent 119
percentage 79, 128
perfect 72, 159
perform 28, 107, 116, 127, 171
performed 110, 278, 282
performers 32, 71, 81
period 30, 171, 252
periodic 107
permission 1, 79
person 1, 9, 12, 16-17, 21, 37-38, 44, 54-56, 68, 79, 84, 89, 107, 118, 122, 150, 154, 163-164, 170, 176, 185, 187, 190-191, 194, 205, 210-213, 216-217, 226-227, 243, 248, 252, 254, 269, 273, 278, 285
personal 3, 8-9, 22, 30-31, 36, 39, 44-46, 48, 57, 61-63, 77, 80, 84, 86, 102, 105, 116, 120-121, 136, 147, 152, 156-157, 159, 165, 170, 176, 178, 180, 183, 186, 203, 208, 212, 230, 232, 234, 240, 246-247, 252-253, 259, 269, 271, 273, 278, 280, 284
personally 8, 152, 164, 210, 212, 237
personnel 241-242
persons 185
persuade 7-9, 127, 175, 212, 275-276
persuaded 168, 210
persuading 147, 286
persuasion 2, 7-8, 10, 201
persuasive 7, 177

Peters 204
petrol 103
philosophy 114, 116, 130
physical 86, 122, 154, 158
picked 225
picture 27, 38, 168, 214, 222-223, 240, 254
piecemeal 50
placed 107, 152
places 95, 231
planned 69, 154, 177, 187, 237, 262, 275
planning 3, 88, 100, 121, 128, 154, 171, 187, 238, 262
played 46, 225, 260, 269
player 252
players 63
Please 21-22, 24, 26, 104, 150, 160, 183, 236, 258, 263, 277, 281
pleased 154, 201, 207, 277
pleasure 66
points 74, 84, 133, 160, 189
policies 13, 111, 129, 274
policy 9, 40-41, 62, 113, 118, 128-129, 174, 183, 201, 235, 239, 273, 286
political 55, 157
politics 155
portable 210
position 30, 34, 37, 46, 50, 54, 65, 67, 69-70, 73, 77-79, 81, 86, 90, 93-96, 115, 117-118, 129, 157, 163, 165-167, 169, 171-173, 175, 181, 186, 190, 219, 223, 234, 236, 238, 249, 256-257, 260, 266-267, 280, 284, 286
positions 51, 132
positive 9, 31, 36, 38, 50, 73, 80, 85, 153, 160, 162, 177, 184, 192, 215-216, 227, 234, 242, 253-254, 256, 264, 270, 279, 285
positively 8, 188, 199
possess 41, 198
possesses 48
possible 7, 40-41, 53, 100, 102, 110, 134, 139, 151, 158, 161, 178, 182, 187, 210-211, 215, 225-226, 258-261, 273-274, 276-277, 280-281, 285-286, 289
postponed 156
potato 204
potatoes 103
potential 11, 57, 77, 92, 131, 133, 135, 144, 151, 161, 168, 170, 174, 183, 197, 215, 222, 242, 248, 266, 269, 272, 282-283, 291-292

powerful 29, 31, 51, 70, 83, 100, 110, 119, 150, 154, 157, 165, 175, 185, 197, 199, 201, 204, 228, 250, 252, 258-259, 263-264, 281, 288
powers 149
practical 12, 172, 181, 285
practice 58
practices 17, 119, 126, 133, 274
precaution 1
precise 203
precision 205
prefer 67, 72, 75, 80, 127, 161, 230, 240, 261
preferably 23
preference 147, 240
preferred 251
premiums 111
prepare 30, 51-52, 93, 121, 139, 143, 186, 210, 213, 251, 275-276, 280
prepared 85, 94, 96, 165, 179, 210
preparing 172, 175
presence 49, 86, 274
present 9, 38, 50, 65, 69, 82, 94, 143, 176, 210, 218, 254, 256, 266
president 13, 113, 121
pressure 20, 34, 95, 98, 143, 152, 185, 270, 272, 274, 286-287, 289
pressured 141, 234, 277
pressures 68, 198
prevent 258
preventing 129
previous 10-12, 14, 17, 23, 26, 28-29, 33-34, 36-37, 41, 49, 51, 53, 61, 63-64, 67, 92, 94, 96, 100, 102, 110, 112, 118, 120, 123, 125-127, 132, 135, 140-141, 145-146, 152-154, 158-163, 165-168, 170, 174, 176-177, 179, 181-185, 187, 189, 194-195, 201-202, 204, 206-207, 210, 212, 214-217, 220, 226-230, 232, 234-236, 239-242, 245-247, 250, 254, 258-261, 265, 268, 270-272, 274-277, 281, 283, 286-287, 291-292
previously 94, 170, 198
primarily 228, 288
primary 7-8, 33, 132, 169
principles 165
priorities 3, 45, 100, 109, 115, 118, 124-125, 146, 158, 179, 190, 198, 243-244, 262, 266, 275, 282, 286-287
prioritize 77, 80, 164, 244, 283

priority 235-236, 247
private 183, 191
privileged 70
problem 2-3, 11-12, 14, 22, 25, 30, 56, 63, 66, 89, 98, 109, 111, 119-120, 125, 127, 131-134, 152, 156-157, 162, 167, 170, 172, 174, 184, 190, 192-193, 205-206, 213, 220, 222-223, 237, 244, 246, 264, 269, 275-276, 279-280, 284
problems 11-12, 25, 56, 70, 94, 96, 111, 116, 126, 148, 161, 165, 170, 173, 177, 182, 192, 195-196, 203, 241, 259, 265, 268, 273, 276, 281, 292
procedure 41, 57, 112, 204, 235, 242, 271, 287
procedures 4, 46, 63, 85, 140, 161, 173, 187, 189, 282, 291
proceed 113, 162
process 4, 54, 61, 77, 106, 114, 118-119, 122, 124, 127, 136, 151, 174, 177, 204-205, 235, 242, 269, 273, 294
processed 127
processes 62, 85, 124, 181, 190, 274
produce 234, 248, 271, 285
product 1, 4, 44-47, 61, 154, 192-193, 222, 231, 273
productive 19, 113-114, 117, 266
products 1, 28, 33, 45, 62, 66
profession 113, 117
professor 91, 162, 254
Profits 47, 80
program 113, 130, 182-183, 226, 273
programs 179, 251
progress 56, 153, 164, 168, 242, 245
progressed 85
project3, 9, 34, 40, 62-64, 69, 76, 79, 84, 89, 97, 101, 114, 118, 124, 126, 129-130, 133, 140, 143, 147, 154-156, 163, 166-169, 171, 173, 176, 180-181, 189, 192, 204-205, 215, 225, 228-229, 235-236, 245, 247, 250, 255, 259-260, 262, 265-266, 271, 287-288, 293
projects 24, 40, 115, 127, 142, 149, 153, 159, 164, 173, 188, 195, 215, 225, 228, 242, 264, 267, 281, 286, 292
promotable 144
promoted 146, 270
promoting 135
promotion 142, 144
prompted 169, 228
propensity 110
properly 47
property 69
proposal 7, 176, 276

proposals 213
propose 40
proposed 52, 63
prospects 193
proudest 35, 39, 285
proved 111
proves 198
provide 23, 43, 53, 177, 190, 227, 257, 279
providing 273
public 45, 104, 114, 143, 177, 181, 237
publisher 1
pulled 290
pulling 98, 173, 189, 251-252
purchase 4, 9
purchased 4
purpose 40
pushed 84
puzzles 203
qualified 231
qualify 249
qualities 16, 38, 41, 217, 255
quality 169, 173, 263, 287
quantity 169
quarter 79
quarters 107
question 3, 14, 54, 81, 137, 184, 218, 273
questioned 174
questions 2, 6, 9, 26, 36, 50, 52, 54, 58, 70-71, 75, 81, 88, 97-98, 147, 197, 218, 222-223, 244, 256
quicker 182
quickly 15, 85, 118, 140, 146, 167, 220, 235, 265, 283, 287, 289, 291
quitting 74
radical 64
rapidly 125, 168, 171, 282, 292
rapport 15, 76, 120, 172, 196, 264, 276
rather 30, 61, 77, 114
reached 134, 137
reaching 201, 228
reacted 118, 199, 259
reaction 167, 235
readily 229
readiness 46

reading 132, 174
realistic 46, 56-57, 67, 69, 72, 78, 81, 92, 96, 113, 137, 155-157, 161, 165, 173, 178-179, 183, 191, 203, 229, 235, 238, 241, 252, 256, 262-263, 265-266, 270, 274, 282-287, 294
realize 30, 194
really 11, 14, 37, 47, 58, 73, 145, 156, 195, 243, 252, 263
reason 8, 24, 40
reasonable 2, 9, 26, 36, 52, 54, 58, 70-71, 75, 81, 88, 97-98, 110, 147, 197, 218, 222-223, 244, 256
reasoning 204, 225
reasons 77, 84
recall 170, 187, 201
receive 41, 120, 132
received 140, 188, 201, 242
recent 8, 10, 12, 16, 21, 34, 55, 68-69, 72, 76, 83, 86, 95, 106, 114-115, 127-128, 133-134, 137, 149, 152, 156-157, 160, 172, 178-179, 184-185, 189, 195, 213, 218, 220, 232, 249, 251, 266-267, 275, 278, 280, 287, 291
recently 4, 156, 182, 187, 190, 220, 228, 264
recognize 192, 281
recognized 47
recording 1
recovery 115
recruiting 131
rectify 207
rectifying 95
reduce85, 161, 232
reduced 107
reducing 119
redundant 92
referees 80
Reference 2, 7, 43
references 43, 174, 236, 295
reflect 255
refrained 280
refund 162
regain 32
regard 100
regarding 75, 293
regardless 142
regards 72
regional 54
regret 39, 254, 272, 280, 291

regular 71, 74, 84, 106, 133, 160, 189, 257
rejected 187
rejection 65
relate 3, 21, 55-56, 155, 187-188, 203, 205, 239
related 142, 148, 172, 184, 197, 255, 266, 281
relates 90
relating 173, 217, 238
relations 196, 269
relative 46
relatively 29, 234, 292
relevant 4, 44, 115, 174, 183, 225, 229-230, 284
reliable 27, 129, 146, 163, 170, 225
religion 7
religious 32
relive 72, 187
relocate 94, 96, 124, 230
remain 11, 80, 126, 152, 203, 215, 235-236
remaining 10, 16, 21, 31, 33-34, 55-57, 67, 72, 89, 95, 135, 147, 150, 155, 184, 186, 198, 234, 243, 254
remember 243
remembered 14, 32, 123
remote 66, 68, 72
remotely 78, 82, 93
remotivate 187, 190
remove 232
removed 243
Removing 2, 19
repeat 184
replace 62
report 63, 131, 212
reporting 120
reports 97, 155, 157, 186, 237, 255, 280, 284
represent 222
represents 103
reproduced 1
repulse 9
requested 1, 18
requests 71, 243, 289
require 11, 64, 142
required 57, 64, 100, 125, 127, 137, 168, 174, 180, 186, 195, 205-206, 209, 227, 230, 240, 250, 254, 256-257, 266, 274, 287
requires 29, 32, 140, 246, 269
research 46, 51, 76, 157, 159, 169, 278

resemble 89
resentment 11
reserved 1, 39, 61, 73, 87, 113, 176, 220-221
resident 211
residual 116
resilience 198
resilient 144, 199
resistance 8, 40, 116, 133, 216, 273, 290
resistant 9, 276
resisted 272
Resolution 2, 11
resolve 11-12, 53, 67, 97, 111, 132, 154, 158, 162, 168, 194, 257, 259, 265, 268, 270, 275, 281
resolved 11, 91, 134, 242
Resolving 3, 208
resonate 9
resources 14, 68, 116, 122, 187, 203
respect 1, 56, 117, 269, 278
respond 52, 74, 110, 128, 130, 152, 184, 246, 290
responded 55, 131, 199
responding 148, 289
response 114, 177
responses 198
responsive 16, 260
restaurant 16
rested 55
restrained 289
result 7, 12, 15, 24, 55, 62, 85, 100, 156, 167, 178, 181, 187, 197, 208, 231, 258, 260, 268, 272, 289
resulted 63, 176
results 50, 73, 85, 160, 177, 192, 234, 242, 270, 279, 285
resume 84, 88
retain 32, 74
retire 170
retreats 237
return 94
revenue 45, 149, 275
reversed 16
review 4, 58, 151, 237, 265, 289
reviews 4, 209, 227, 256, 287
revised 111, 129
rewarding 260
rewards 180

rights 1
rigors 29
ringing 77
rising 116
riskiest 229, 268
rounding 77, 152, 161, 234, 276
routes 143
routine 63, 181
sacrifice 287
sacrifices 150, 180, 183
salary 2, 18, 51, 53, 67, 74-76, 78, 80, 85-87, 90, 135
salient 199
satisfied 56-57, 63, 148, 154, 218, 289
satisfy 31, 52
savings 275
saying 243, 280
scales 103, 105
scares 67
schedule 67, 72, 75, 115, 160, 229, 244, 247, 262, 266, 279
scheduled 257
scheduling 2, 100, 109, 235-236, 247, 266
school 21, 32, 34, 38, 93, 104, 113, 173, 187, 195, 223, 225, 233, 251, 255, 268, 279
schooling 249
schools 169
science 229
scissors 103
scratch 22
screw-up 145
searching 31, 209, 256, 265
second 25
secondary 203
seconds 50, 107
seeking 18, 128
seemed 125
seemingly 31
seized 167
Select 161, 168
selected 223
Selecting 3, 263
selection 51
sellers 1
selling 10, 46, 62, 93, 160

seminar 115, 211
senior 34, 145, 199
sensitive 28, 141, 185, 234
sentence 222-223
separate 12
Sequencing 50
serious 11, 150
service 4, 61, 162, 193, 207
services 1, 9, 66, 222, 231
servicing 113
serving 34
setback 68
setbacks 197, 283
setting 2-3, 46, 54, 121, 137, 157, 175, 205, 243, 283-284, 294
settings 54
settle 208, 273, 280
settling 276-277
several 30, 117, 126
severe 154
sexual 130
sharing 43
short-Fire 238, 267
should 7, 9, 36, 47, 51-52, 68, 72, 77-78, 124, 130, 144, 147, 150, 158, 184, 188, 203-205, 218, 222, 249, 253, 255
shoulder 150
shouldn 150
shouldnt 110
showed 269, 278
showings 80
shrunk 107
side-Fire 225
signature 129
similar 8, 12, 17, 25-26, 34, 41, 44-45, 54, 58, 62, 68, 77, 80, 83-84, 111, 114-115, 119, 125-126, 128, 135-136, 142-143, 145, 149, 155, 157, 159-160, 168, 172, 180, 182, 188, 191-192, 194, 199, 210-211, 213, 221, 226, 228, 251-252, 265, 267, 275-282, 285
simple 14, 27, 93
simply 4
sincerity 53
sinful 232
Singapore 194
single 32, 36, 65, 81, 86, 106, 137, 180, 256, 258

situation 8, 11-12, 14, 19-20, 24, 29, 31-32, 44, 51, 53-54, 61, 64, 67, 72, 75-76, 80, 85-86, 89, 92, 96, 100, 118, 120, 124-126, 130, 133, 140, 143-146, 150-152, 154-158, 163, 168, 171, 177, 180-181, 184, 187, 189, 193-194, 197, 201, 205, 207-208, 210-212, 214-217, 226, 229-230, 232, 234, 236, 239-240, 242, 254, 258-259, 261, 263-268, 270-272, 274-275, 278, 282, 285, 287, 289-290
situations 19, 55, 57, 96, 110, 117, 130, 152, 154, 166-167, 199, 211, 273, 276, 290
skeptical 9
skilled 61, 186
skillful 184
skills 2-3, 12, 25-26, 34, 41, 54, 58, 62, 68, 83-84, 100, 111, 114, 117, 125, 135-136, 142-144, 149, 155, 168, 172, 182, 188, 191, 207, 210-211, 213, 221, 226, 228, 239, 247, 251-252, 265, 276-277, 279-280, 282, 285
smarter 31
Smarts 21
smells 13
smooth178
smoothly 122
social 31, 69-70, 86, 114, 124, 127-128, 153, 203, 205
societies 82
software 129, 179
solicit 123
solution 12, 51, 63, 172, 181, 285
solutions 115, 229
solved 63, 116, 120, 131, 174, 220, 279
solving 3, 11, 22, 66, 70, 111, 125, 134, 156, 192, 203, 206, 220, 222, 276
somebody 7
someone 8, 15, 25-26, 29-30, 32, 37-38, 49, 51, 53, 71, 77, 83, 86, 90, 96, 98, 122, 127, 129, 134-135, 147, 159, 163, 166, 173, 175, 185, 189, 201, 204, 212, 215, 226, 242, 246, 251-253, 256, 258-261, 264-265, 267, 269, 271-272, 274, 278, 283, 286
something 7, 14-15, 31, 63, 77, 86, 90-91, 93, 105, 134, 137, 148, 159, 167, 172, 180-181, 183, 185, 190, 192, 210, 222, 226, 237, 250-251, 263, 280, 284, 286, 290-291
Sometimes 10-11, 16, 63, 100, 171, 242
Sooner 289
sounds 147
source 12, 91, 268
sources 33, 132, 169
speaker 25

speaking 291-292
special 2, 40-41, 74, 79, 90, 100, 120, 125-126, 130, 169, 176, 194, 199, 216, 235, 239, 241, 243, 257, 259, 261, 281
specific 8-9, 11-12, 14, 22, 30-34, 40, 49-50, 52, 54, 56, 61, 63-64, 66, 68, 74, 79, 89, 98, 102, 109, 111-112, 114-115, 118-120, 122-123, 125-127, 131-134, 140, 148-149, 152-153, 156-157, 159-160, 162, 167-168, 170, 172-176, 178-179, 183-184, 187-190, 193-195, 201-206, 211, 213, 215-217, 220, 222-223, 225-228, 234-237, 241-242, 244-246, 250, 253, 255, 257, 264, 269, 272, 274-276, 279-281, 284, 289-290
speech 213, 275
speeches 139
spending 13
sponsor 41
Sporting 65
spouse 29, 126, 172, 184
square 106
stability 7, 282
stable 11, 16, 18, 20-22, 25-26, 28-30, 32-34, 38, 40-41, 54, 62, 64-66, 72-74, 76-78, 80-83, 85-89, 91-94, 97-98, 109, 111, 114-117, 119, 121, 125, 127-128, 130, 140, 142-143, 145-146, 148, 152, 155-161, 163-165, 167-168, 170, 172-174, 177-178, 180-181, 183-185, 187-190, 192-193, 195, 201, 204-205, 208, 217-219, 221, 229-233, 236, 238, 241, 249, 252-257, 267-268, 270-271, 277-278, 280, 284, 287, 290, 292
stacked 31
staffs 285
stalled 118
stamina 29
standards 3, 45-47, 172, 241, 281, 294
started 3, 71, 167, 181, 195, 220, 228, 264, 282
starting 22, 156
startup 21
stated 9, 40-41, 113, 118, 128-129, 174, 183, 201, 235, 239, 273, 286
statement 39, 50, 61, 205, 253, 278
statements 178
states 106-107
stations 103, 106
status 124, 127, 153
staying 88
stimulate 203
Stones 193

stories 10, 136
strangest 15
strategic 3, 100, 121-122, 137, 165, 238, 276, 285
strategies 13, 234, 244, 272, 277
strategy 118, 128, 223, 229, 274, 292
strength 16, 33, 54, 117, 121, 123, 169, 198, 267
strengthen 50, 212, 282
strengths 2, 67, 70-71, 88, 92, 98, 117, 149, 160, 162, 166, 175, 191, 202, 218, 237, 249, 269
stress 2, 20, 28, 30, 32, 34, 145, 178, 185
stresses 12, 182, 265
stressful 20, 77, 141, 158, 187, 276, 282
stretch 147, 163
strong 9, 13-14, 47, 74, 189, 260
stronger 71, 192, 204
structure 64, 128, 269
structured 37, 47, 62, 250
struggled 76, 116, 261
student 172, 220
subject 83, 89
subjects 34
subscribe 36, 249
subsequent 21, 29, 55-57, 67, 71, 77, 91, 100, 104, 186, 232, 277, 282
succeed 80, 284
success 7, 12, 30, 60, 63, 67, 72-73, 84, 112, 120, 125, 129, 135, 142, 165, 171, 173, 183, 186, 193, 201, 215-216, 228, 231-232, 235-236, 241, 265, 267, 271, 289
successes 114
successful 16-17, 29, 50, 56-57, 73, 86, 112, 117, 121, 148, 164, 167-169, 188, 191, 212-213, 216, 226, 241, 255, 258, 262, 267, 275, 277, 279, 288-289
suddenly 247, 279
suffered 171
sufficient 171, 234, 252, 285
suggest 257
suggested 127
suggestion 62, 181, 232
suited 162, 190
summer 34
super-Fire 16
superhero 104, 149, 250
superior 47, 127, 210, 289

superiors 140, 242
superpower 79
supervise 87, 165
supervised 114, 226, 263
supervisor 35, 111, 124, 152-153, 159, 162, 164, 166, 170, 188, 212, 241, 257, 263, 265, 269, 275, 289
supplier 120
support 9, 14, 40-41, 45, 49, 111-113, 132, 142, 199, 203, 227, 232, 270, 274
supported 49, 113, 121
supporting 129
supports 233
suppose 9, 21, 124-125, 134, 192
supposed 17
survivor144
suspect 45
sustain 15, 72, 115
switch 92, 103
switches 103
system 40-41, 44, 164, 170, 175, 177, 236
systematic 177
systems 2, 44, 75, 122, 132
tackle 136
taking 37, 40, 56, 156, 182, 245, 250
talked 43, 197-198, 237
talking 25, 53, 281
target 46, 165, 235
taught 44, 211
teaching 34
teammate 74
teamwork 3, 54-56, 126, 177, 258
technical 58, 68, 112, 131-133, 139, 151, 165, 168, 186, 188, 191, 206, 211, 213-214, 236-237, 240, 263, 265, 268, 281, 289-292
techniques 38, 116, 158, 174, 189, 203, 256
technology 61-63, 66, 229
tenant 76
tendencies 14
tennis 105, 107
terminal 120, 157, 265
terminate 124
terrific 8
territory 91
tested 12, 182, 265, 276, 289

thefts 30
themselves 168, 214
Therefore 217
Theres 124, 251
things 8, 13, 21, 31, 33, 38, 40, 54, 56-58, 63, 81, 85, 96, 100, 121, 148, 153, 159, 162, 165, 168-169, 174, 178-179, 185, 193, 195, 201, 212, 229, 231-232, 241, 244, 253, 262-263, 266, 268-269, 279, 284
thinking 2-3, 34, 44-45, 51, 55, 61, 64, 203, 205, 222, 254
thinks 185
though 289, 293
thought 61-62, 65, 122, 130, 164, 204, 212, 269, 286
thrilled 169
thrive 22, 198-199
thriving 33, 198-199
through 7, 11, 34, 45-46, 61, 68, 80, 90, 117, 122, 126, 143, 150, 171, 204-205, 210, 216, 235, 269, 292
throughout 1, 66, 117, 147
thrown 107
ticket 194
timely 101, 242
timetable 165
together 102, 126, 186, 273, 277
toilets 98
tolerate 141, 154
tomorrow 29, 74
totally 177
toughest 83, 98, 102, 116, 147
Toughness 3, 197
toward 55-56, 177, 183
towards 46, 56
trademark 1
trademarks 1
training 41, 120, 123, 130, 203-204, 226, 251, 257, 273, 281
traits 36-38, 81, 254, 256
transfer 41
transition 226, 282
translate 242
travel 83, 87, 156, 180, 250, 254
traveled 29
traveling 33
travelling 74
trends 68, 117, 230

tribal 15, 45-46, 51, 58, 64, 73, 114-118, 121, 129, 131-133, 143-146, 164, 173, 179, 185, 203, 205-206, 238, 262, 267
trouble 276
troubling 57
trusted 111
trusting 163
trying 110, 157, 166, 184, 193, 201, 216, 259, 271, 290
turned 121, 232
twenty 262
typical 66, 182, 189, 191-192, 282
typically 64, 100, 239, 260, 269, 279, 283, 285
ultimate 197
ultimately 36, 198, 253
unaware 193, 269, 280, 284
uncertain 47, 96, 145, 183, 198-199, 238, 275
undergoing 144
understand 40, 124, 134, 166, 211, 213, 271
understood 176, 210, 269, 285
undertook 228
uneasy 13
unethical 110
unexpected 146, 162, 187, 241
unfair 115
unforeseen 262, 266
unguarded 126
uniform 47, 58
unions 168
unique 11, 21, 63, 90, 93, 135, 164, 206, 221, 236, 257, 259, 279, 282, 286
United 106-107
university 75, 82, 87
unload 103
unpleasant 28, 210, 289
unpopular 9, 55, 120, 132, 176, 215, 239, 242
unrelated 193
unreliable 121
unsettled 171
untapped 203
unusual 62-63, 139, 242, 277-279, 284, 286
urgent 71
useful 10, 201, 209
utilised 13
utilize 9, 69, 234, 277

vacation 8, 21, 106
valuable 47, 61-62, 64, 68, 71, 130, 229-230, 284
valued 49
values 2, 22-23, 28, 33-34, 49, 54, 104, 133, 211
variable 15-17, 44-45, 62, 163, 185, 194, 212, 216, 261, 281
Variety 2, 24, 49
various 9, 87, 121, 123, 293
vendor 118, 120, 189
verbal 210, 213
verify 79, 271
Version 295
versus 154, 171, 244
viable 208
virtual 41, 43, 73, 75, 79, 93, 96, 123, 129, 136, 161, 179, 197, 199
vision 73, 148, 173, 238, 287
vocabulary 25
voicemails 71
volatile 145
volunteer 102
waiting 30, 61
wanted 201, 217, 270
warrant 265
warranty 1
weakness 17, 33, 85, 87, 121, 255
weaknesses 2, 67, 74, 76, 86, 92, 98, 149, 160, 175, 191, 219, 249
weather 14
website 90
weekends 32, 81
weight 98, 135, 173, 189, 251-252
welfare 154, 156
werent 169, 174
whether 114, 116, 122, 171, 222
willing 17, 30, 52, 87, 94, 96, 124, 156
windowless 103
winning 14, 47
within 40-41, 131, 179, 221
without 1, 28, 56, 61, 87, 103, 105, 204-205, 232, 234, 285
withstand 29, 198
workday 133
worked 29, 31, 44, 62, 69, 71, 85, 94, 120, 123, 129-130, 132, 157, 164, 167, 181, 190, 214-215, 222, 227, 236, 260, 272, 284-285

worker 112
workers 30
working 7, 12, 23, 30, 33, 36, 38, 43-44, 66-67, 72-73, 76, 80, 82, 87-88, 93, 97, 114, 117, 123, 130, 134, 149, 156, 164, 171, 185, 188, 194, 215, 217, 230-231, 240, 252-254, 257-258, 260, 268, 273, 281
workload 129, 174
workplace 13, 145, 188, 202, 246
workshops 237
workspace 86
Worried 15, 255
worrywart 57
wouldn39, 149
wouldnt 7, 173, 176
writing 4, 104, 130, 183, 191, 210, 269
written 1, 175, 210-213
x-foot 131
yellow 107
yourself 7, 14, 30, 38-39, 53, 55-56, 60, 65, 68-69, 76, 82-84, 86, 92, 95, 100, 118, 121, 129-130, 145, 150, 152, 164, 167, 172, 176, 181, 183, 185, 188, 190-191, 201, 204, 219, 221, 232, 235-236, 240, 244, 251, 254, 256, 261, 265, 274, 285, 289-290

Made in the USA
Las Vegas, NV
30 March 2023

69889577R00193